INVISIBLE MONEY

Family finances in the elect

Jan Pahl

The POLICY PRESS

First published in Great Britain in 1999 by
The Policy Press
34 Tyndall's Park Road
Bristol BS8 1PY
UK

Tel no +44 (0)117 954 6800
Fax no +44 (0)117 973 7308
E-mail tpp@bristol.ac.uk
http://www.bristol.ac.uk/Publications/TPP

© The Policy Press and the Joseph Rowntree Foundation 1999

Published for the Joseph Rowntree Foundation by The Policy Press

ISBN 1 86134 158 X

Jan Pahl is Professor of Social Policy, University of Kent at Canterbury.

The **Joseph Rowntree Foundation** has supported this project as part of its
programme of research and innovative development projects, which it hopes will
be of value to policy makers and practitioners. The facts presented and views
expressed in this report are, however, those of the author and not necessarily
those of the Foundation.

The statements and opinions contained within this publication are solely those
of the author and not of The University of Bristol or The Policy Press. The
University of Bristol and The Policy Press disclaim responsibility for any injury
to persons or property resulting from any material published in this publication.

The Policy Press works to counter discrimination on grounds of gender, race,
disability, age and sexuality.

Cover design by Qube Design Associates, Bristol
Photograph kindly supplied by www.johnbirdsall.co.uk
Printed in Great Britain by Hobbs the Printers Ltd, Southampton

Contents

List of tables and figures

Tables

Figures

Acknowledgements

I am very pleased to have an opportunity to thank the Joseph Rowntree Foundation, which funded this study, and especially Barbara Ballard for all her advice and support. The University of Kent also gave a small grant at the crucial pilot stage. The Advisory Group has been immensely helpful and stimulating and I am very grateful to those who gave so generously of their time and expertise: they included Julie Baden-Powell-Jones, Carole Burgoyne, Jackie Goode, Helen Finch, Elaine Kempson, Heather Laurie, Alan Lewis, Elizabeth Phillips and Kit Ward.

This research could not have taken place without the participation of those who came along to the focus groups or who agreed to be interviewed in their homes. They gave us information about a very private aspect of their lives and I am extremely grateful to them all. In order to maintain the confidentiality of what they told us, in the pages that follow all names, and some identifying details, have been changed.

I should like to thank most warmly those who have helped with the collection and organisation of the data. They included Social and Community Planning Research, who were responsible for organising the focus groups: my thanks especially to Helen Finch and Kit Ward. The interviewees were recruited by the Independent Fieldwork Company. The interviews were carried out by Robert Ireland, Marion Kumar, Hilary Legard and Sharon Neal: I am very grateful to them for the professional way in which they did their jobs. The tapes were typed up by Pat Hedges and her colleagues, Jill Relton and Lynne Jones, while Barbara Wall helped with data entry: I very much appreciate all their efforts on behalf of the study.

I also want to thank the ESRC Data Archive, at the University of Essex, and the Office for National Statistics, for making the Family Expenditure Survey available to researchers and for being so helpful in answering our queries. Lou Opit carried out all the statistical analyses of the Family Expenditure Survey and contributed enormously to the study in many different ways. His death in May 1998 caused great sadness, and this book is dedicated to his memory, with my love.

Summary

This study set out to explore the ways in which individuals and couples are using new forms of money, such as debit and credit cards, smart cards, telephone and Internet banking. The aims of the study were:

- to examine the extent to which new forms of money constrain or enhance the access that individuals have to the money that enters the household in which they are living;
- to consider whether access to money held electronically is related to other characteristics of individuals, such as income, employment status, education, age, gender, spending power and access to goods and services;
- to draw out the implications for those responsible for policy making, in terms of the payment of benefits, wages and salaries, the availability of credit facilities and the growth of inequality, both within and between families.

The study involved three different research methods. Quantitative data came from re-analyses of the Family Expenditure Survey interviews with 3,676 couples. Qualitative data came from seven focus groups, which took place in different parts of England, and from face-to-face interviews with 40 couples, in which husbands and wives were interviewed separately and privately.

Key findings

1. The 'electronic economy' is developing at great speed. Cash and cheques are used less than they used to be, and credit and debit cards much more. Telephone banking is increasingly popular, but Internet banking is still regarded with suspicion.
2. For many people cash is still 'real money', and they are less confident about using what they see as 'invisible money'.
3. Those who are affluent and technologically confident may enjoy and be excited by new forms of money; these 'enthusiasts' experience the thrill of the new, but they are also privileged consumers.
4. For those with lower incomes or less secure jobs, credit cards can be the source of much anxiety; some may respond by being careful about not getting into debt, but those who are more carefree may not be able to resist the dangers of easy credit.

5   Many people are finding it harder to budget, because debit cards do not provide a record of what was spent and the time-scale of credit card repayments may not match the income and expenditure patterns of families.

6   Loyalty cards are much more likely to be used by women than men, and by those on middle incomes. High-income consumers tend to scorn them, while poor people tend to use shops where they are not offered.

7   There are clear patterns of exclusion from the electronic economy, which reflect education, income, employment status, gender and age. Those who are 'credit rich' tend also to be 'information rich' and 'work rich'; those who are 'credit poor' tend also to be 'information poor' and 'work poor'.

8   Education is particularly important in giving people the confidence to use new forms of money. Individuals are having to go 'shopping for money', and this means that advantages accrue to those who have developed the necessary literacy and numeracy skills.

9   Putting benefit payments on to smart cards may lessen the danger of theft but can also create problems, since these are the families most likely to use cash for all financial transactions and least accustomed to using credit and debit cards.

10 New forms of money are changing the ways in which families control and manage their finances. Individuals in couples can use new forms of money to conceal spending from each other, or to maintain a higher standard of living than their partners.

11 Half of the couples who took part in the focus groups and interviews had both joint and sole bank accounts, while one quarter only had joint accounts and one quarter only had sole accounts. The banking arrangements of couples can reveal a great deal about the nature of the relationship.

12 Men make more use of new forms of money than women do, and tend to dominate the use of new technologies such as Internet banking: this is changing the gender balance of financial power within families.

13 The scope of social policy should extend to cover the financial services sector and the implications of changes in the electronic economy for the welfare of individuals and families.

Implications for social policy and for financial services

The study had implications for a range of areas of social policy. These included:

- combating the financial exclusion of some families and neighbourhoods;
- developing alternative sources of credit, for example, through credit unions;
- recognising the problems that new forms of money may pose for those with low incomes and fewer years of formal education;
- extending access to financial education and financial advice services;
- taking account of research on the control and allocation of money within the family in policies related to marriage and divorce.

Source: Forester (1987, p 230)

ONE

Introduction

Since the first credit card was launched in 1966, there have been dramatic changes in the ways in which ordinary people hold, manage and spend their money. Credit cards have been followed by store cards, debit cards, loyalty cards and smart cards. Banking by computer and telephone began in the 1980s, with an accelerating expansion in the use of electronic banking services throughout the 1990s. All these developments, described here as 'new forms of money' or the 'electronic economy', are making money increasingly invisible. Are they altering the ways in which individuals and couples control and allocate their financial resources?

The original aims of this study were:

- to examine the extent to which new forms of money constrain or enhance the access that individuals have to the money that enters the household in which they are living;
- to consider whether access to the electronic economy is related to other characteristics of individuals, such as income, employment status, education, age, gender, spending power and access to goods and services;
- to draw out the implications for those responsible for policy making, in terms of the payment of benefits, wages and salaries, the availability of credit and the growth of inequality, both within and between families.

The idea that underpins the study is that new forms of money may be creating a set of filters which enhance or constrain the access that individuals and households have to the market. Those who are credit-card-rich must not only be creditworthy, but must also be confident of their ability to manage the technology and to repay the debts that may be incurred. Those who are credit-card-poor may have failed to pass the scrutiny of the credit reference agencies, or may simply lack the confidence to use the new forms of money. Those who have gained the right to a credit card though the creditworthiness of others, such as non-earning wives who have a second card on their husband's account, may feel that their spending is constrained by the need to account for the items on the monthly statement.

Telephone, computer and Internet banking are still relatively new, but all the evidence suggests that those who have access to these facilities may in the future be able to save money and gain access to a wider range of goods and services. Thus, managing and spending money is no longer simply a matter of making the cash go round, but an electronic activity which is shaped by complex social and economic processes. The effect is to create a global financial system which privileges some individuals and households and from which others are partly or completely excluded.

The growth of new forms of money

New forms of money can take many different forms, so it may be helpful to begin by outlining the main features of each. The various types of plastic card have been usefully summarised by the Credit Card Research Group (1998).

Credit cards can be used to make payments and to withdraw cash up to the cardholder's agreed credit limit. A magnetic strip identifies the cardholder when the card is used. Each month a statement is sent to the cardholder listing the amounts spent over the previous month and asking for payment of a minimum amount of the outstanding bill. Interest is charged on all transactions unless the full amount is paid by the due date; some cards also have an annual fee. All credit cards are linked to an international card scheme, such as MasterCard or Visa.

Charge cards, such as American Express, are used in the same way as credit cards, except that the bill must be paid off completely each month. They usually have higher annual fees than credit cards, particularly if they are gold or platinum charge cards, and offer a wider range of other services.

Store cards or retailer cards are similar to credit cards, but each card can be used only in the shop or store by which it was issued.

Loyalty cards are also issued by particular stores; examples include Safeway's Loyalty card, Sainsbury's Reward card, WH Smith's Clubcard and Boots' Advantage card. As far as customers are concerned, they offer bonus payments or other incentives, which are calculated as a proportion of the total sums spent; as far as retailers are concerned, they collect valuable information about customers' shopping patterns and make it possible to target sales more effectively.

Debit cards were first introduced in 1987, and are sometimes described as 'Pay Now' cards, to distinguished them from 'Pay Later' credit cards. Debit cards can be used to make purchases in the same way as a credit card, but the payment is taken directly from the cardholder's bank account. The details of the payment appear on the customer's bank statement. The two main debit cards used in Britain are Switch and Visa Delta. Both also have schemes where each transaction has to be authorised electronically to ensure that there is enough money in the account, so that the user cannot go overdrawn: these cards are called Solo and Electron, respectively.

Automated teller machine cards (ATM cards) allow users to use the 'hole in the wall' provided by banks. The cardholder has to type in a Personal Identification Number (the PIN), and can then withdraw or pay in money, check balances and move money between accounts. Most ATM cards also function as debit/credit cards and cheque guarantee cards.

Smart cards, which are also known as chargeable cards or electronic purses, represent the future in the world of plastic cards. Each card contains an embedded microprocessor chip which makes it possible to load money on to the card from the holder's bank account, or from a terminal or telephone. It can then be used like cash in any retail outlet that has the terminal required to read the information held on the card. Examples of smart cards are the Mondex card, issued by MasterCard, and Visa Cash. Smart cards can do all that credit cards and debit cards can do, but can also hold money in different currencies and can store information such as passport and identity details, supermarket loyalty points and health records (Brown-Humes, 1998c). In the future smart cards will be linked to computer operating systems, making it possible to access electronic cash and on-line shopping from the home computer (Cole, 1999, p 12).

There are striking differences between countries in the use made of plastic cards and in the types of card most favoured by users. The differences between France, Germany, Italy, Spain and the United Kingdom were documented in a report produced by the Credit Card Research Group (1997). At the end of 1996, the UK had the highest proportion of cards per head of the population, with 1.1 cards per person, compared with 0.9 card per person in Germany and just 0.2 card per person in Italy. In general, the countries of northern European had a higher number of cards per head than the countries of southern Europe, with Italians in particular being great users of cash as opposed to cards. There were also differences in terms of the types of card used. While debit cards dominated in France and Germany, there was a more even split between credit and debit cards in Italy, Spain and the UK. However, the ownership of cards was not necessarily reflected in the frequency with which they were used. Despite the high number of cards held in Germany, they were used relatively sparingly, compared with France, where the smaller number of cardholders used their cards more frequently. So in 1995 the average number of payments per card was 79 in France, compared with 6 in Germany and 32 in the UK (Credit Card Research Group, 1997, p 4). The reasons for these differences are unclear and warrant further investigation.

By 1998 there were around 1,300 different brands of credit cards in the UK, most of them issued by one of the 30 main card issuers (Credit Card Research Group, 1998).

The growth of new forms of banking

The growth of plastic cards has been paralleled by the expansion of electronic banking. Indeed, in the near future the two trends are likely to merge, when it becomes possible to swipe a credit card though a slot on a home computer to pay for goods and services ordered over the Internet. There are three main forms of electronic banking.

Telephone banking involves having a bank account that is designed to be accessed by phone, and that allows customers to check balances, set up direct debits, pay bills and switch money between accounts. In the UK the telephone banking revolution began with the launch of First Direct in 1989. Since then the number of people banking by phone has grown from 2.5 million in 1994 to 8.7 million, or 24 per cent of all current account holders, in 1998 (Brown-Humes, 1998a, p 20). Telephone banks are open in the evenings and at weekends, and even throughout the night, and some offer higher interest rates on savings because there are no expensive high street branch banks to be maintained.

Computer banking involves the use of specially designed software, which is installed on a home computer and connected to the bank's computer through a modem and telephone link. The growing number of banks that offer electronic services claim that they have been more popular than expected, but there is still customer resistance to the fees that most banks charge for computer access and to the narrow range of services currently on offer (Mackintosh, 1998, p 20).

Internet banking lets customers connect to their bank over the Internet, using standard browser software, such as Netscape or Internet Explorer. The connection should be possible from any computer in the world, so long as it is linked to the Internet, unlike the situation with computer banking, which can be done only from the machine on which the software has been installed. Anxieties have been expressed about the security of this system (Mackintosh, 1998, p 20). However, there is no doubt that ways will be found to offer greater security, and when this is the case Internet banking is expected to expand its scope and coverage. A further thrust will come from the expansion of the services available in the major supermarkets: the development of supermarket banking and of Internet shopping means that the home computer could play an increasingly important part in the management of personal finances (Brown-Humes, 1998b). One enthusiastic user of on-line banking was reported as saying:

> It has really made a difference. I can keep an eye on what my wife has been spending and I know what is coming in on a daily basis over and above the last statement. It helps me keep my account in order. (quoted in Wolf, 1998, p 12)

Remarks such as this remind us that all the new ways of holding, managing and spending money have been launched into the complex world of personal and household finances. In classical economic theory the household is conceptualised as an economic unit, and the assumption is made that households can be regarded like individuals in any analysis of their economic behaviour. However, sociological research on the intra-household economy has revealed a more complex picture, as Chapter 2 will show.

TWO

Background to the study

Previous research on new forms of money

There is a growing literature on the development of new forms of money and on the implications of this for the financial services sector and for consumers. The changes that have taken place are often presented as a revolution:

> Where credit cards made lending quicker and easier, and debit cards aimed to replace the cheque, the electronic purse is the potential replacement of cash itself. If it is successful it will revolutionise banking and commerce. (Gosling, 1996, p 75)

However, it is not certain whether the changes will benefit consumers. Will they become the "kings" in the new financial market-place or will they remain essentially "peasants", in the words of Burton (1994, p 94)? One study of financial services and the consumer concluded that:

> It is clearly the case that financial service producers in Britain have become more consumer oriented. However, it would be inaccurate to conceptualise these trends as a reformulation of the producer–consumer relationship whereby consumers have become more powerful than producers, as some commentators have argued. The number of financial institutions from which consumers can purchase financial services has declined. The number of banks and building societies has fallen.... Information technology has given producers an important method of controlling consumer behaviour via credit referencing and credit scoring. (Burton, 1994, p 111)

One characteristic of the literature on new forms of money is that typically consumers are conceptualised as individuals, rather than as one of a couple or as part of a household. Thus economists have focused on the individual credit card user, on the development of user profiles, and on the exploration of broader economic issues. (See, for example, Feinberg et al, 1992; Burton, 1994; Crook et al, 1994; Brito and Hartley, 1995; Duca and Whitesell, 1995). At the level of macro-economics there has been interest in the implications for the money supply of the increased use of credit cards (Laidler, 1993; Begg et al, 1994).

The Centre for Economic Psychology at the University of Bath has investigated the ways in which financial services are perceived by consumers, and has shown that the consumers of financial services are becoming more demanding, less loyal and better informed (Lewis et al, 1997). Researchers at Brunel University have documented a continuing concern among consumers about privacy and security in the electronic market-place (Hine et al, 1997). Work at the University of Keele has examined the implications of the growth of 'plastic money' (Worthington, 1998).

In the field of social policy, research on new forms of money has been concerned in particular with issues related to access to credit and credit card debt. For example, work at the Policy Studies Institute has analysed the use of credit cards. It has shown that the use of credit cards rises with income, so that in 1989 only one in seven of the poorest households had a credit card, compared with three quarters of the most affluent (Berthoud and Kempson, 1992). Credit card default is often the result of job loss, small business failure or changes in family circumstances (Ford, 1988, 1991; Kempson, 1994; Rowlingson and Kempson, 1994).

The implications of these changes have been documented by the Personal Finance Research Centre at the University of Bristol, which has provided evidence of the extent of financial exclusion (Kempson and Whyley, 1999). This research has shown that in the late 1990s two out of ten households did not have a current bank or building society account, three out of ten had no savings at all and about the same proportion had not had access to consumer credit facilities in the previous year. The situation was exacerbated by the fact that people who lacked one type of financial product had an increased likelihood of being without other products as well. Some households were particularly likely to suffer from financial exclusion. These included lone parents, single people, households headed by someone who was unemployed or disabled, and members of ethnic minority communities. The researchers concluded that:

> ... the consequences of not having access to key financial products
> – a bank account, consumer credit, savings or insurance – are

much more serious than they were in the past. Being part of a
small minority who are outside mainstream financial services creates
a new set of difficulties ... the options are far more costly and
often unregulated. (Kempson and Whyley, 1999, p 22)

The changes taking place in the financial services sector have increasingly
been the subject of political debate. Shortly after taking office, the
Labour government announced a new system for financial services
regulation, and in 1997 concentrated powers in a new body, called the
Financial Services Authority. This is responsible for informing the
public about the financial products that are available, encouraging the
development of more flexible products and ensuring that relevant
information is available for consumers (Treasury Select Committee,
1999a, p v). The government also initiated the Financial Services and
Markets Bill, which was published in July 1998.

The minutes of the Treasury Select Committee which considered
the new provisions for financial regulation made it clear that financial
exclusion was expected to be of concern to the Financial Services
Authority. Patricia Hewitt MP, then Economic Secretary to the Treasury,
giving evidence to the Select Committee, said:

We want to see a financial services industry in this country that is
offering all consumers or potential consumers the advice, where
that is appropriate, and the product that they need to meet their
particular needs. (Treasury Select Committee, 1999b, p 79)

She expressed concern about the difficulties faced by individuals without
bank accounts and communities without branch banks, and went on to
mention the task force on credit unions and banks which has been
established within the Treasury.

Evidence was also given to the Select Committee by the Banking,
Insurance and Finance Union (BIFU), which represents workers
employed across the finance sector. This suggested that access to basic
financial services is increasingly part of social well-being in a modern
economy, and concluded by proposing the idea of 'financial citizenship':
"BIFU believes that access to financial services is essential to full
participation in the community" (Treasury Select Committee, 1999b, p
90).

Debates such as this make it clear that the scope of social policy is
changing. The traditional focus on health and social care, social security,
education and housing is no longer enough. The financial services

sector has the power to affect the welfare of citizens quite profoundly, and the extension of the regulatory state means that the divide between the private and public sectors is no longer so rigid. In this context, it is important that social policy analysts turn their attention to the ways in which ordinary people think about, and use, financial services.

However, most of the literature on new forms of money has been concerned with either individuals or households. It has not taken account of the complex financial negotiations that take place between individuals within households, a topic on which there is an increasingly sophisticated literature.

Previous research on money and marriage

Research on the control and allocation of money within the household has shown that couples control and manage their money in many different ways. Some couples pool all their income, typically in a joint bank account, and attach considerable importance to financial equality. Other couples maintain independence in financial matters, dividing responsibility for the payment of joint bills and attaching importance to privacy and autonomy in financial matters.

Some couples give overall financial control to one partner or the other, while others divide finances into separate spheres, making each partner responsible for specific areas of spending. The most recent evidence, from the British Household Panel Survey, suggests that about half of all couples pool their incomes and share management of the pool. In about a third of couples finances are managed by the wife, while in about one sixth they are managed by the husband, typically with a housekeeping allowance being transferred to the wife. Finally, a small but growing number of couples hold and manage their money as though they were still two separate individuals (Laurie and Rose, 1994; Laurie, 1996).

Previous research has shown that the ways in which couples manage their money reflect a range of different variables. When money is short and making ends meet is hard, women typically manage finances on behalf of the household. At higher income levels, employment status becomes important. If only the husband is in employment he tends to control the money, often delegating the management of a part of it to his wife. The higher the proportion of the household income contributed by the wife, the more likely it is that she will control finances and have power in financial decisions (see, for example, Wilson, 1987; Brannen and Wilson, 1987; Morris and Ruane, 1989; Pahl, 1989, 1995; Vogler and Pahl, 1993, 1994; Laurie and Rose, 1994).

Ideology is a crucial variable, but one whose effect is often difficult to quantify. The ideology of equality within marriage probably had as much effect on the spread of the joint account as did the increase in women's employment, but it is hard to disentangle the two variables. The increase in independent management of money may reflect the individualisation that has been identified as a feature of late 20th century life (Beck and Beck-Gersheim, 1995). Another related change has been towards greater diversity in the structures of family life. Whereas 50 years ago a majority of the population grew up in two-parent families, with the parents remaining married to each other throughout the life span, the increases in divorce and remarriage mean that family finances have become more complex. Individuals may have financial responsibilities to more than one household, and may have to choose between competing claims on their resources (Burgoyne and Morison, 1997).

Most previous research on financial arrangements within marriage has implicitly conceptualised money as cash, while acknowledging that in many cases the cash is actually held in a joint or individual bank account. Research on the ways in which couples use bank accounts has suggested that the development of more complex forms of money management is leading to a lessening of collective financial arrangements (Cheal, 1992; Treas, 1993). Even though opening a joint account is often a symbol of togetherness, many individuals within couples also maintain their own separate accounts, and these are legally available only to those whose names are specified as having access to them. Qualitative work carried out for the British Household Panel Study has shown that setting up banking systems, such as standing orders, feeder accounts and transfers between current and deposit accounts, tends to be a male activity, and can have the effect of reducing the access that women have to the financial resources of the couple (Laurie, 1996).

This brief review of the existing literature suggests that most research on the control and allocation of money within marriage has paid little attention to the implications of new forms of money. Conversely, most research on new forms of money has ignored the social and economic processes that shape financial arrangements between individuals within households. An exception is the research that has been taking place in Melbourne, Australia, at the Centre for International Research on Communication and Information Technologies (CIRCIT). This has suggested that developments in banking technology are altering the ways in which couples manage their money. Different forms of money can be used for different kinds of payments, in a way that expresses not only what is being bought but also who is making the purchase. Singh concluded: "The connections between banking and marriage are so critical that electronic banking technologies are altering the way money is managed and controlled within marriage" (Singh, 1997, p 166).

The study reported here began with an interest in the control and allocation of money within marriage, and then moved on to explore the ways in which new forms of money are altering, or being incorporated into, financial arrangements within households.

Methods of the study

Money is a sensitive and private subject. All researchers know that asking people about their finances can be more intrusive than asking about sexual relations. In addition, this study was essentially exploratory. Therefore it seemed important to use a variety of research methods, partly in order to throw the investigative net as wide as possible, and partly to gain experience about the acceptability and validity of different methods, in a way that might benefit future research on the topic.

Three different sources of data were used, in order to gain both quantitative and qualitative information about the issues that were being explored. First, analyses of the Family Expenditure Survey (FES) provided quantitative data about 3,676 married couples, which could be generalised to a larger population because of the nature of the survey. Second, seven focus groups took place, involving 59 individuals living in five different parts of England. Finally, face-to-face interviews were carried out with 40 couples, in order to develop a more qualitative understanding of the ways in which individuals and couples managed their finances and made use of new forms of money. Men and women were interviewed separately and privately. Further details about the methods used in the study are given in Appendix A.

In the chapters that follow, different sources of data are combined to illuminate particular topics. Chapter 3 is concerned with the many different forms that money can take and with the ways in which people talk about, and use, new forms of money. This chapter draws mainly on the focus groups, but also presents some data from the interviews. Chapter 4 moves on to look at patterns in the use of credit cards and at the ways in which some individuals and groups are being excluded from the electronic economy. Financial exclusion is explored using data from the FES, and the findings that emerge are illustrated with quotations from an argument that took place in one of the focus groups. Chapter 5 is concerned with the ways in which new forms of money are being incorporated into the financial arrangements of married couples. It illustrates the data from the FES with case studies from the interviews, and adds some stories from the focus groups about the financial secrets that exist in many marriages. Chapter 6 explores changes in banking and uses data from the focus groups and interviews to show how banking arrangements can offer a revealing insight into family relationships. Finally, in Chapter 7 some of the policy implications of the study are discussed, and suggestions are made for the directions that policy might take in the future.

THREE

Mix and match in money management

The great variety of new forms of money means that most people have a choice in how they pay for the goods and services they buy. At the supermarket till, at the garage or in the travel agency, they may be deciding between cash or cheque, credit card or debit card. How and why are these decisions made? What are the patterns in the use of particular forms of payment? What meanings do individuals attach to the different forms that money now takes?

Choosing how to pay

In the years between 1985 and 1997, there were profound changes in preferred methods of payment in the United Kingdom. Figure 1 shows that in 1985 the majority of payments were made by cheque, with credit cards being used relatively rarely and debit cards not at all. Over the following years payments by cheque lost ground to automated payments, such as direct debits and standing orders, while debit cards overtook credit cards. In 1998 the number of payments made by credit card exceeded the number made by cheques and other automated methods (Inman, 1999).

Figure 1: Non-cash transactions, by method of payment

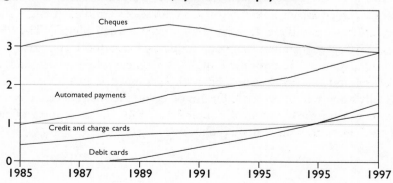

Source: Association for Payment Clearing Services
(ONS, 1998, p 115)

Previous research has suggested that people prefer to use different forms of payment for purchases of different cost, with a move away from cash towards credit cards as cost increases, except for very expensive items which tend to be paid by cheque. Thus, a survey of 2,000 adults, carried out for Girobank, showed that cash was the preferred means of paying for items costing under £10; for purchases of £100, cash was preferred by 25 per cent of those surveyed, down from 28 per cent a year earlier, while credit cards were preferred by 43 per cent, up from 39 per cent a year earlier. For purchases costing £1,000 cheques remained the first choice for 46 per cent, compared with 33 per cent who said they would use a card and 10 per cent who would use cash (Graham, 1997).

Everyone who took part in the face-to-face interviews was shown a list of items and asked to say whether they usually paid for each item by cash, cheque, credit card, debit card, direct debit, standing order or some other means. Given that only 40 couples, that is 80 individuals, were involved in the interviews, their answers cannot be treated as representative of the population as a whole, but they do give an idea of the way in which people select different forms of money depending on the purchase which they are making. Table 1 shows the responses when interviewees were asked, 'How do you usually pay for [this item]?' It shows that cash is still an important medium of exchange, but that for some areas of spending, such as on household goods, clothes and holidays, credit cards have overtaken cash. Household utilities, such as gas and electricity, tend to be paid for by direct debit or standing order, with cheques still being used for some of these payments.

The patterns given in Table 1 are similar to those found in the FES data, which identified the items for which credit cards were most likely to be used. These were household goods, holidays, and clothes (Pahl and Opit, 1999). Items that were rarely or never bought with a credit card included tobacco, alcohol, repairs to the house, and gambling. (The settlement of gambling debts by credit card is actually illegal.) The FES analysis had also shown that some goods, such as food, childcare and school expenses, are typically bought by women, while others, such as alcohol and the costs associated with cars and car maintenance, are usually bought by men. So Table 1 is based on the answers given by the women who took part in the interviews, with the exception of the starred answers, where men's replies were used.

Table 1: Forms of money used to purchase different items*

	Cash	Cheque	Credit card	Debit card	DD/SO‡	NA§
Food	22	3	10	9	-	-
Heating costs	7	13	-	2	22	1
Household goods	10	4	20	1	6	2
Holidays	10	10	21	2	-	3
Alcohol†	29	2	9	2	-	3
Car costs†	22	3	10	5	2	4
Childcare/school	11	3	2	3	2	21
Man's clothes†	13	3	19	9	-	1
Woman's clothes	16	4	18	10	-	-
Children's clothes	10	3	5	5	-	19

Notes: *Total number = 40 couples: interviewees could give more than one answer.
† Man's answer used; all other answers were those of women.
‡ direct debit, standing order.
§ Not applicable, not bought.

To know something about how and why people decided to use a particular form of money, we turned to data from the focus groups.

Cash and cheques

All the focus groups spent quite a lot of time discussing different methods of payment. These discussions underlined the many meanings attached to money. Economists have traditionally regarded money as 'fungible', so that one unit of wealth is substitutable for any other: a pound is regarded as a pound no matter where is comes from and how it is held (McCloskey, 1987). However, there is a growing literature which questions the accuracy of this assumption and shows how the social meaning of money can vary according to its source, the purpose for which it is to be used and the person entitled to use it (see for example, Winnett and Lewis, 1995; Wilson, 1999; Zelizer, 1994). Evidence from the focus groups showed not only that different forms of money had different meanings, but also that the same form of money could vary in the meanings attached to it by different individuals. Invisible money could feel very different from 'real money'.

Some of the most vivid and contradictory accounts of the meaning of money came in discussions about the use of *cash*. Some people used very little cash, while for others it constituted the main form of payment.

Attitudes to cash seemed to be partly a consequence of how an individual was paid, but they also reflected social class and gender. On the one hand, more men than women were paid in cash and used cash as their main form of payment, but on the other hand, more men than women claimed that they rarely used cash at all.

There was a subgroup of middle-class men who were disdainful of cash and took pains to make their stance clear to other members of the focus groups: it almost seemed to be a matter of status not to carry cash, or to carry just enough 'for chocky bars'. A sales manager in Leeds said:

> "I've never got any cash. I always use cards – even things like cigarettes and what have you I tend to put on the card. I do quite a lot of business in London and down there if you entertain somebody or go out for a drink you just put your credit card behind the bar."

The wife of a chartered surveyor said, "My husband never carries cash – he's like the Queen".

By contrast, there was another group – typically working-class men – who used cash as their main medium of exchange, and expressed doubts about other forms of money:

> "If I haven't got thirty quid in my back pocket, I don't think I've got any money. Maybe that's going back to the days when I couldn't afford to have money in my back pocket – I just like to have that bit of cash in me back pocket." (Man aged 50, self-employed builder)

In general, women were likely to take a pragmatic approach to deciding how to pay, but even among them, working-class women were more likely to prefer cash. Some were nostalgic for what they defined as 'real' money:

> "When I first started work in 1970, we used to get paid weekly – the little old brown envelope and the holes in it – and everybody got paid real money. People paid their rent or their gas bill or whatever. I'm sure if we all got paid in real money, we'd perhaps still be paying our bills.... It's too easy to spend money that perhaps you haven't got. I mean you've all got credit cards, debit cards, you get an overdraft, you just spend what ever you've got and pass the cards over. Whereas if it's real money, you can't do it. So the

banks have encouraged us to overspend." (Woman aged 43, sales assistant)

When they discussed *cheques*, many of the participants in the focus groups were quite dismissive, often mentioning cheques only to stress how few they used. Out of the 59 people who took part in groups, 18 claimed never to use cheques, while only 13 said that they used cheques quite often. There was no difference between those over and under 40 in this respect, but men were in a substantial majority among those who said they never used cheques: writing them out was described as "too much of a faff" or "in the ark".

Those who liked and used cheques often did so because they allowed a record of spending to be kept; typically, these were working–class women responsible for making ends meet on relatively low incomes:

> "I can write out all my cheques; they all go down as I use them. And at the end of the week, I write down all what I've paid out and what I've got left and I'm quite happy and satisfied. When I used my Delta card, I kept on forgetting to put it down and I'd think 'Oh dear, I spent a bit more than I should have this month'." (Woman aged 53, care assistant)

Sometimes it seemed as if cheques offered a way into managing invisible money, more tangible than electronically handled money, but more modern than cash:

> "My son is quite into money management. He's joined every sort of bank to get the freebies; I think he's got six accounts. He's 13. I didn't encourage him to open so many accounts, but when his grandparents send him cheques, he can pay them straight into his account. I think it's quite good for them to learn management of it early, if that's going to be the way of progress and they're never really going to see cash." (Woman aged 49, bilingual secretary)

These findings are in line with market research on the use of cheques. The use of cheques declined from 25 per cent of all non–cash transactions in 1990 to just 8 per cent in 1994: this form of payment has been described as "suffering a lingering death" (Gosling, 1996, p 141).

Credit and debit cards

By contrast, credit and debit cards have grown enormously in popularity over the past 20 years. Table 2 shows that between 1990 and 1996 there was an increase in the percentages of individuals holding all types of card; however, increases were particularly marked for ATM and debit cards. Men were more likely than women to hold every type of card, except the retailer cards issued by stores to their customers.

Table 2: Plastic cards held by women and men in Britain (1990 and 1996)*

	1990		1996	
	Women (%)	Men (%)	Women (%)	Men (%)
ATM debit card	47	53	74	80
Debit card	35	45	59	66
Credit/charge card	34	43	37	46
Retailer card	18	12	28	19
Any plastic card	67	73	81	86

Note: *% of adults aged 16 and over holding each card.
Source: *Equal Opportunities Commission (1997)*

By 1999 nearly half of all adults in the UK held a credit card and eight out of ten a debit card (Inman, 1999, p 27).

The focus group discussions about credit cards revealed a variety of different attitudes. Some people were enthusiastic about all new forms of money, while others were more sceptical. For some, credit cards offered a means of controlling their finances more efficiently, while for others they provided a way to maintain spending patterns, at least for a time, even though their finances were essentially out of control.

Enthusiasts talked about credit cards not just in terms of what they offered, but in terms of meanings and symbols:

"I love Visa. I mean, where else can you go with a bit of plastic – leave England at six o'clock in the morning, be halfway round the world at twelve o'clock the following day and still carry on using it? It's superb." (Man aged 36, commercial fleet manager)

Some were envious of the privilege and status which they thought particular cards attracted:

"A friend of mine's got the American Express Gold Card, and I've often thought I'd like to be in that bracket, because when he goes places, he's treated like royalty. You know, when he goes to buy a new car, whereas I have to think, 'Oh God, I can't afford it, it's going to be hire purchase or something like', he goes in and it's 'Thank you very much, sir, there's the keys, two years warranty, sir'. Oh yes.... " (Man aged 41, lecturer in further education college)

Those who were sceptical about credit cards were often concerned about the possibility of getting into debt, and felt that they were safer with a debit card than a credit card. Many felt that other forms of money allowed them to maintain a better check on the state of their finances, like the following woman:

"I'm extremely frugal and cautious with money.... We don't have a regular income – he's self employed – so we might go three or four months with no money, so then whatever you run up (on a credit card) is a bit of a shock: its got to be paid for. I tend to use Switch for my big shop in Sainsbury's once a week. I go to Asda normally on a Monday morning and I often write a cheque for that. Then I'll have cash for the little shops, the butcher, the greengrocer, children's things."

Interviewer: "How do you decide 'This time I'm going to write a cheque'?"

"I think to myself, 'Goodness, I've spent quite a lot on Switch this week'. Because its easy to forget Switch, so I write on the stubs. Then you've got so many minuses on the stub it gets filled up and I think I've got to start off with a fresh stub and write another cheque – that's about as much as it is really." (Woman aged 39, part-time secretary)

The focus groups revealed profound differences between those who used credit cards to control their spending and those whose credit cards allowed them to be out of control financially. This is how one discussion went:

"I think you've got to be sensible with them. I mean I'm – we're sensible with ours. We know how much to sort of go to and

every month it's paid off. I never get charged interest on it."
(Man aged 48, cable supervisor)

This remark was followed by envious murmurs round the group of "Lovely, I'd love to do that", and "I always get charged interest", and "It's like a dream that is". These comments encouraged another 'sensible' response:

"I've only been overdrawn once on it and that was a mistake. If you use a Switch card it's taken out directly, it's all sorted and you know where you are. But [with a credit card] you've got six weeks and then you get this huge bill at the end. But my husband persuaded me that you get your profile points and you get six weeks in which to sort it out and it's better. I've got used to it now, but I have to pay if off every month." (Woman aged 41, no paid work)

However, the other members of the group returned to the debate:

"But if you're gonna do that, why have it? I mean if you've got the cash, why have a credit card? I know you get your six weeks' free interest and you get your points and what have you, but my idea of a credit card is – I haven't got the money! Go on, whack it on there, I'll worry about that later." (Man aged 48, manager)

Another added:

"It's a sod it card, isn't it? That's what it is. You want to do something, you haven't got the money and you think, 'Oh, we'll go and do it anyway'. 'Cos you've got a credit card, so you can just go and do it. 'Sod it, we'll do it anyway'." (Woman aged 43, sales assistant)

All the focus groups produced examples of the cutting up of credit cards, often vividly described as landmarks in the financial history of individuals and couples. Cutting up cards was mentioned spontaneously by about a quarter of those who took part in the focus groups, with no differences between men and women, but with an over-representation of people in social class C1 among those who had cut up cards. It seemed that cutting up cards was characteristic of those for whom getting cards was easy, while paying back the debt incurred could be difficult.

Some people cut up their own cards, while others, predominantly men, cut up their partners' cards. For one man, his profound lack of belief in the principle of paying interest on debts added to his resentment, though the problems originally began when he was made redundant:

> "We had a credit card and we done something really silly. We'd still buy the food and all this spending exactly the same. I was literally working myself into an early grave. I had four sort of part-time jobs – I was coming home at two, three o'clock in the morning. We sat down and found it was this bit of plastic. We was working for a piece of plastic. I know it's your debt, but you get a magic debt of say a hundred pound and then someone'll put fifteen pound on it and that used to make me so angry. So it was destroyed."

> *Interviewer:* "Did it take you long to destroy your card, or was it an easy decision?"

> "Oh no, it was an easy decision.... When I think I'd paid something like a hundred pounds to this imaginary person, who was getting my money every month, I thought, 'That's my money; why are you pinching something you're not working for?'" (Man aged 41, lecturer in further education college)

For some people credit cards were simply too dangerous; this was especially so for those who were unemployed. One of the interviews involved a young couple in their 20s, living on social security with their small daughter in a high rise block in West London. The woman had run up big debts with a credit card in the past, and had eventually cut up her card, but they now budgeted entirely in cash. She said:

> "If we need anything – the money's in the drawer. So we go to the drawer, get the money out. All our money's accounted for. It's a lot easier. You know, like you've got little pots – you've got your rent, got your electric, got your gas, got yourself. If we have got spare we put it away in the drawer until we've got a reasonable amount to go and spend."

Her husband was also wary of the dangers of credit cards:

> "Some of my friends have got credit cards and, you know, they

throw it around and then they can't go out for six months because they've got to pay back what they've been flash on. It's easy money. I mean if you've got two and a half grand limit on your card, it's like saying you've got two and a half grand in the bank, isn't it, even though you've got to pay interest on it?"

When asked how he would describe people who had lots of cards, he said:

"Oh, flash, Flash Harry. It's either gonna be a right poser, or someone who's got nothing and is trying to be something that they're not."

Discussions in the focus groups often became quite complex and technical, with those who were better informed sharing some of what they knew with those who knew less. Sometimes it seemed as if knowing about money was another forum for the exercise of consumer skills, and another arena for competition, especially among men. Listening to these discussions, it seemed as though *shopping for money* was becoming an activity in its own right.

Smart cards and loyalty cards

Smart cards, or chargeable cards, have been much trumpeted in the financial press. But how are consumers responding, and what part do they play in family finances? All the focus group participants and all the interviewees were asked about these cards. However, most people had not heard of them, and when the idea was explained, they were not particularly interested. The exceptions were Swindon, where the Mondex card was coming towards the end of its trial, and Leeds, where the VisaCash card had just been introduced.

None of the eight people who took part in the Swindon group had a Mondex card and all were scathing about the idea. One man said:

"I looked into it, 'cos I work in the town centre and it seemed a very good idea and at work we have a little card that you can load with money and can get your coffee out of it and it sort of takes it off. It's like a smart card, same as Mondex. But they charge £6.50 a month for Mondex: so you pay to spend your own money." (Man aged 36, commercial fleet manager)

Other comments were equally dismissive: "Mondex you have to put money into it, whereas with Switch you just use it", and "I don't know anyone personally that's got a Mondex card", and finally and most disparagingly, "There's a real stigma about having a Mondex: it's an embarrassment to say you have a Mondex card in Swindon".

However, in Leeds the VisaCash card was meeting a different reception. Of the 16 people who took part in the two focus groups held in the city, six had one of the new cards and most people had heard of the scheme. In the all-women group only two people were using the cards, one of whom worked in the financial services sector. Her remarks implied that the card was seen as some sort of fashion accessory:

> "The places we would go to on a lunch time or the wine bars, all these places for lunch, its very much the in thing. In the wine bars in town, where all the suits go on a lunch time – if you haven't got one, don't bother going!" (Woman aged 38, underwriter)

Several women in the group were concerned about the implications of the new cards for family finances. One woman said, "You'll have to trust each other more than you used to". Others said:

> "You would have to say, 'Well, I'm taking £20 out this month: do you want any out and we will do it together.' And deduct it from your account. And then you would know where you were." (Woman aged 31, sales assistant)

> "Yes, like if you had a joint account you would have to make sure that you only drew the same amount on the card as you would have done if you had been going for cash." (Woman aged 26, Inland Revenue officer)

The women's group also agreed that men would be more likely to use the new cards than women, an idea that was confirmed when half of the eight men in the all-male focus group had acquired the new VisaCash cards. Again they made links with the fashion industry:

> "It's the way everybody will be in five years. In five to ten years there won't be any cash."

> *Interviewer:* "But will it necessarily be VisaCash?"

"Well, it could be anything, but VisaCash is first and best dressed – there's no option. I mean the payoff's phenomenal – you don't have to queue. I went to WH Smiths and I bought a load of stuff. I went straight to the machine – meanwhile there's a queue a mile long waiting to pay cash. I stuck my VisaCash card in the machine, it took the money off me, I was away. People were looking at me, like 'Who the bloody hell are you, jumping the queue?' But the woman said 'You got a VisaCash card, up you come'." (Man aged 44, Internet consultant)

The all-male group did not mention the implications for family finances of the new chargeable cards, a topic that came up spontaneously in the women's group. By contrast, the men emphasised that the cards would become really useful only when they were accepted in pubs, newsagents, car parks and so on.

All the focus groups, however, were eager to talk about *loyalty cards*, and about the pleasure of apparently getting "something for nothing" when they made a purchase and points were added to the card. It seemed that this was a topic that united people, while discussion of credit cards emphasised the distinctions between the affluent and the poor. In general, women were more enthusiastic than men: "Well, they don't do the shopping, do they?" one woman commented. Men were more likely to make remarks like, "You just need a bloody great wallet – there's so many of them". However, loyalty cards did provide opportunities for individuals to turn 'our' money into 'my' money. One woman said, "I'll get my Air Miles and escape", while a man joked, "I stick my card into her purse so she thinks she's using her own!"

The idea that loyalty cards enabled poor people to feel they had a foothold in the credit card economy was challenged by the data from the interviews. Almost all the couples had loyalty cards, with the exception of two very poor couples from Leeds, who did not have cards because the places where they usually shopped did not offer them but concentrated on keeping prices as low as possible. However, the interviews confirmed the gender division: women were much more likely to own and use a loyalty card than men, and were less likely to be scathing about the whole idea. The attitude of many women was expressed by this cook:

"They're a good thing, because you've gotta go and buy the food anyway. I get them out twice a year. I get them out at Easter, some of them, and that buys all my Easter eggs for my grandchildren, and then come Christmas, Sainsbury's pays for my Christmas."

Loyalty cards came in for a great deal of criticism as "a scam", "a con" or "a load of rubbish". Men, such as this computer salesman, were more likely to be critical than women:

> "I see it as being insulting that they would think that I think we're getting real benefit because they're giving me points. Why don't they just knock a penny off the products, or something like that. Give me something real – I don't want to mess about collecting points."

The parts of the interviews concerned with loyalty cards underlined the class and gender divisions that run through patterns of consumption. The affluent scorned them as a commercial trick, while the very poor shopped where they were not offered: between these two extremes people got "something for nothing", either with pleasure or with a degree of resentment. Women's responsibility for doing the family shopping was reflected in the fact that only one tenth of the women who were interviewed did not have a loyalty card, compared with two thirds of the men. When asked about loyalty cards one man, who was very much in control of finances in the household, commented "that's her department".

Patterns in the use of new forms of money

Table 3 represents an attempt to make sense of the complex mass of data produced by the focus groups. The table is divided between those with high and low incomes and those with positive and negative attitudes to new forms of money (NFM). It suggests that different subgroups face different financial issues, make use of different forms of money and have different definitions of cash.

Table 3: Attitudes to new forms of money (NFM), by income level

	Attitudes to new forms of money generally	
Income level	**Positive**	**Negative**
High	**1 Enthusiasts**	**2 Sceptics**
	Issues: life-style; 'shopping' for money; technophilia	*Issues:* security; privacy in financial matters; technophobia
	Use: all NFM; telephone and computer banking	*Use:* cheques; also credit and debit cards; store cards
	Cash: low status	*Cash:* 'real' money
Low	**3 Careful/carefree**	**4 Excluded/discredited**
	Issues: control of finances or being out of control	*Issues:* poverty; juggling debts and commitments
	Use: all NFM; loyalty cards	*Use:* cash; loyalty cards
	Cash: another form of money	*Cash:* main form of money

The *enthusiasts* tended to be interested in all new forms of money, and with relatively high incomes they were able to acquire whatever credit cards they wanted. They were well informed about the different types of card and took pride in sharing this information. As they talked, it sometimes seemed as if new forms of money were part of a more general life-style, which involved keeping up to date with fashions in technology and in the world of finance. This group tended to be eager to find out about telephone and computer banking. They saw themselves as financially astute: one man had 17 building society accounts as a way of optimising his chance of benefiting from any bonus payments to shareholders! As evidence of their technophilia, members of this group enjoyed being scathing about the inconvenience of cash. There tended to be more men than women among the 'enthusiasts' and more younger than older people.

The *sceptics*, by contrast, felt doubtful about the benefits of new forms of money, while having the income to be eligible for every type of credit card. This was the group most likely to express concern about giving credit card details over the phone or Internet, and it was they who most valued the personal service given by branch banks. They were most likely to make payments by cheque, and though they used credit and debit cards, they still thought of cash as "real money". Some felt quite uncertain about what might be the "best buy" in the money market. This group contained a higher proportion of middle-aged and elderly people, and was predominantly middle class.

Lower-income households with positive attitudes to new forms of money were divided between the *careful* and the *carefree*. Limited incomes meant that for both groups the control of finances was a real issue and information about new forms of money could be the best protection against financial disaster. Used carefully, credit cards offered a way to smooth out the peaks and troughs of demands on the budget, but this demanded considerable self-control if the aim was to pay off the account each month. For this reason, many people in the 'careful' group preferred debit cards to credit cards, some of them explaining that the system meant that they would not be 'allowed' to go overdrawn at the bank. (In reality, this is true only for some debit cards.) The 'carefree' approach was epitomised by the idea of the 'sod it' card, to be used when no other source of money was available. This group seemed to assume that their credit limit represented the amount that they could reasonably spend and they were resigned to paying interest on the debt. If their income dropped, the 'carefree' could face real financial problems, to which one solution was the cutting up of the offending card. Another consequence of a drop in income could be longer-term exclusion from creditworthiness, and a descent into the world of the discredited.

Those who were *excluded* were also literally the '*discredited*', to use the term suggested by Kempson and Whyley (1998). They belonged to that group of the population who are not considered eligible for credit by banks, building societies, credit card companies and credit rating agencies. Clearly, poverty was a major issue, involving a relentless struggle to juggle debts and commitments of one sort or another. In these circumstances cash typically became the main form of payment. For those without credit cards, the loyalty cards offered by the main chain stores could be quite important. Not only did these cards appear to offer something for nothing, but they also allowed the holder to feel part of the card-holding society. There was evidence of this in the focus groups, when the topic of loyalty cards often produced the most animated and friendly discussion of the evening. As might be expected, those who were excluded from the electronic economy were most likely to be unemployed, or in low-paid and insecure jobs.

Conclusions

The patterns that emerged from the focus group discussions suggested an increasing polarisation in terms of access to the electronic economy. The 'enthusiasts' were rich in financial terms, but they were also 'work-rich', in that typically they belonged to households with more than one earner, 'credit-rich', in that their credit rating was secure, and 'information-rich', in that they felt confident about their ability to manipulate the financial market-place to their own advantage.

At the other extreme, those categorised as 'excluded' were also 'work-poor', typically living in households without a regular earner, 'credit-poor', in that it was hard for them to get any sort of loan, and 'information-poor', in that they did not understand the rules of the new world of personal finance. In the focus groups these individuals were sometimes quite tentative and lacking in self-confidence, while in the interviews they often had to have the different types of debit and credit cards explained to them. There is certainly a need for more accessible financial education and advice services, but it is also important to recognise how much of a burden it can be for consumers to be faced with the complexity of the electronic economy.

Qualitative data, such as that produced by the focus groups, can only suggest patterns and stimulate ideas. It seemed that income and employment status were particularly important in shaping patterns in the use of new forms of money, but larger numbers would be necessary in order to confirm the picture. For a more quantitative analysis, we turned to the FES. Chapter 4 describes the results.

FOUR

Inclusion and exclusion in the electronic economy

The focus group discussions had suggested that there might be patterns in the use of new forms of money. Trying to identify those patterns raised many questions. Was it just a matter of taste and personality? Were attitudes to credit cards a product of individual psychology, of the differences between 'enthusiasts' and 'sceptics', between the 'careful' and the 'carefree'?

However, previous research had suggested that socio-economic variables might also be important. In that case, was the crucial variable income, which would mean that better off people could afford to make light of credit card bills that would be a burden on the budgets of the less well off? Or was employment a more important variable, so that those with secure, full-time jobs felt more confident in using credit cards than those whose jobs were less secure? Or was there some other variable that shaped patterns in the use of credit cards? This chapter will be concerned with questions such as these, with the aim of identifying patterns in the extent to which individuals and couples were included in, or excluded from, the electronic economy.

Patterns in the use of credit cards

The Family Expenditure Survey (FES) provided an opportunity for testing out the ideas about the use of credit cards that had come from the focus groups (ONS, 1996). Since the study was concerned primarily with how new forms of money were being incorporated into the financial arrangements of families, we based the analyses on the expenditure diaries which were filled in by married couples: in the year in question (1993/94), there were 3,676 such couples, drawn from every part of Britain.

Discussion in the focus groups had suggested that two aspects of employment were particularly relevant to whether or not people used credit cards. These were, first, the employment status of women, with a distinction being made between full-time, part-time and no employment, and, second, household employment status, with a distinction being made between 'work–rich' and 'work–poor' households. In order to examine the effects of these two aspects of employment, a variable was created which combined the employment situations of both the man and the woman. This involved recoding the employment variables given by the FES to make six broad *household employment categories*. (For further information about the categories see Pahl and Opit, 1999.) The categorisation involved taking account of the employment status of both partners, so that the sample was divided as follows:

- both employed full–time
- husband employed full–time, wife employed part–time
- husband employed full–time, wife not in paid work
- wife main earner (husband may be retired or disabled)
- both retired
- both unemployed.

The expenditure diaries that are kept by all those who take part in the FES require them to record if a credit card is used to make a purchase. Table 4 shows the percentage of men and women in each employment category who had used a credit card to make a purchase during the two weeks when they were filling in the expenditure diaries. The statistical significance of each row of the table was tested using a chi–squared test, with *N* being the total number of households recording expenditure on the item in the two–week period.

Table 4: Percentages of individuals using a credit card to make a purchase by household employment categories*

| Household employment categories | Credit card used to make a purchase | | | | |
| | Men | | Women | | |
	%	N	%	N	Significance[†] p <
Both full-time	42	350	41	349	n/s
Full-time/part-time	42	356	35	304	0.085
Full-time/no paid job	37	256	25	170	0.001
Woman main earner	24	66	23	63	n/s
Both retired	21	174	14	119	0.003
Both unemployed	6	9	7	12	n/s
All	33	1,221	28	1,017	

Note: *Total number = 3,676 couples.
[†]n/s = not significant.

Table 4 suggests that between a quarter and a third of all those who took part in the survey used a credit card over the two-week period, with men being more likely than women to have used a card. Differences in the use of credit cards were associated with differences in employment status. When the man and the woman were both in full-time employment they were equally likely to have used a credit card. However, women in part-time employment were less likely, and women without employment very significantly less likely, than their employed husbands to have used a credit card.

The table highlights the exclusion of unemployed people from the credit card economy, with only a very few individuals in this category using a credit card during the two weeks. This is consonant with research on access to credit more generally, which has shown that low-income households find it hard to obtain credit; if they have to borrow, they tend to be forced to contact more expensive money lenders than the typical credit card company (Ford, 1988, 1991; Rowlingson, 1994; Kempson et al, 1994).

Retired people were the other group that appeared to be relatively excluded from the credit card economy. This may be partly a result of low income and lack of creditworthiness. But it may also be a consequence of a lack of financial confidence in new forms of money and of a general mistrust of getting into debt. There was a significant difference between men and women among retired couples, which may reflect differences in income, a lack of confidence by women in using new technologies or a tradition of male dominance in financial matters. It may be that for some couples the retirement of the man is associated with a handover of power to him from the woman, in an attempt to compensate him for his loss of earning power.

However, Table 4 lumps together some very disparate individuals. For example, a situation where both partners were in full-time work might have been a 'dual career' couple, in which two highly educated individuals held well-rewarded jobs. Alternatively, both partners could have been in full-time work because their lack of education and low incomes meant that two earners were necessary to maintain the family: in other words, they were a 'dual job' but not necessarily a 'dual career' couple. Similarly, where women were without paid work this could be a brief temporary break from employment for a mother with young children, or it could be evidence of a longstanding traditional pattern in which the man was expected to be the breadwinner while the woman concentrated on homemaking.

Explorations of the FES data had suggested that the use of credit cards was statistically associated with a number of different personal, demographic and financial characteristics of the individuals in the sample. Clearly, such variables were interrelated in a complex way. A statistical cluster analysis was used to create a new classification of individuals which would examine the relationships between education, income and employment status. The aim was to identify clusters of individuals with common characteristics and to investigate patterns of credit card use for each cluster. Further information about the cluster analysis and about the characteristics of the individuals in each cluster is given in Appendix B; details of the statistical techniques are available in Pahl and Opit (1998).

Cluster analysis of credit card use

In order to examine the interlocking effects of the different variables, the computer program was asked to define six clusters, basing the clusters on age at the end of full-time education, the income of each partner, and the employment status of the couple. The cluster analysis was carried out separately for men and women, so the totals in each cluster are not exactly the same for each sex. Table 5, which cross-tabulates the clusters with the employment categories used in Table 4, shows that the cluster analysis illuminated many details that had been concealed within the household employment categories.

Cluster 1 contained a high proportion of individuals who were retired or living in households with no paid work. The majority of both men and women in this cluster had ended their education at age 14 or 15 and incomes were uniformly low. (For details about age at the end of full-time education and income, see Table A1 in Appendix B.) For most of the households in this cluster social class was not recorded in the FES. (For details about social class, see Table A2 in Appendix B.) So a typical member of cluster 1 had left school at the minimum age and was *unemployed* or *retired*.

Cluster 2 contained many couples where the woman either was in part-time employment or did not have a job. In this cluster women's incomes were substantially lower than those of the men, despite their similar levels of education. Typically, the head of the household was classified as being a skilled manual worker, though this cluster also contained some retired people. So the typical couple in cluster 2 was a *skilled manual worker whose wife had part-time or no paid work*.

Table 5: Six clusters by household employment categories, by women and men*

Household employment categories	Cluster number					
	1	2	3	4	5	6
Women						
Both full-time	9	85	216	54	305	188
Full-time/part-time	12	346	29	190	212	69
Full-time/no paid work	86	331	5	227	24	15
Woman main earner	75	31	62	7	90	9
Both retired	658	106	19	30	27	8
Both unemployed	125	17	1	7	1	-
Total	**965**	**916**	**332**	**515**	**659**	**289**
Men						
Both full-time	11	75	194	59	330	188
Full-time/part-time	14	331	26	202	223	62
Full time/no paid work	93	319	2	228	32	14
Woman main earner	84	23	62	7	89	9
Both retired	653	107	13	30	37	8
Both unemployed	124	17	1	7	2	-
Total	**979**	**872**	**298**	**533**	**713**	**281**

Note: *Total number = 3,676 couples.

Cluster 3 contained many couples in which both partners were in full-time employment, with the relatively low income levels of the men being balanced by the relatively high incomes of the women. This suggested that these were couples where having two earners was necessary in order to make ends meet. The women tended to have had more years of education than the men. In terms of social class, these were households where the 'head' was likely to come from social class II or be a skilled manual worker. This combination of characteristics suggests that cluster 3 might be described as *middle income, dual job couples.*

Cluster 4 contained many households where the man had a full-time job, while the woman had no paid work or only a part-time job. This cluster was characterised by medium levels of education for both men and women. However, there was a substantial gender gap in terms of income, with men typically earning much more than women. In terms of social class, the 'head of household' was likely to be classified as social class I or II. So a typical couple in cluster 4 might be characterised as *middle class, with a breadwinner husband and a homemaker wife.*

Cluster 5 was a cluster in which most women were in full-time or part-time employment, and in which many were the main earners for the households in which they lived. Typically, it contained individuals who had relatively low educational levels, with most people leaving school at age 15 or 16. Among men especially, their low educational levels were translated into relatively low incomes, with most 'heads of household' being classified as social class IIIM. By contrast women's incomes were at medium levels for women in the sample, suggesting that many had jobs classified as social class III, non-manual. So cluster 5 could be described as the *low income, dual job couples.*

Cluster 6 contained the most highly educated individuals in the sample, with both men and women typically having completed some years of higher education. The effect of this showed in the relatively high income levels for both men and women, and in a social class classification that placed the majority in social classes I and II. Table 5 shows that both partners tended to be in full-time employment. Typically, these were *high income, dual career couples with professional jobs.*

The cluster analysis inevitably simplified the complexity of reality. However, it did make it possible to group households according to some key structural variables. The analyses presented here showed how much households varied when the education, income, social class and employment of both partners were taken into account. As we shall see, these variations were reflected in very significant differences in the use of credit cards.

Table 6 gives the percentages of individuals in each cluster who had used a credit card during the two weeks during which the expenditure diaries were being kept. The most striking variations were between the different clusters: these were highly significant for both women and men. Thus, at one extreme, 68 per cent of men in cluster 6 had used a credit card to make a purchase, while at the other extreme only 8 per cent of women in cluster 1 had used a credit card during the two weeks when the survey took place. As we have seen, cluster 6 contained the most highly educated and best paid couples in the sample, while cluster 1 was predominantly composed of people who were retired or unemployed.

Table 6: Percentages of women and men using a credit card to make a purchase over a two-week period, by cluster*

	Cluster number					
	1	2	3	4	5	6
Women						
% who used a credit card	8	20	40	42	23	63
Total number	965	916	332	515	659	289
$p < 0.0001$						
Men						
% who used a credit card	11	24	33	52	22	68
Total number	979	872	298	533	713	281
$p < 0.0001$						

Note: See Appendix B for a description of the clusters.

Credit card use was highest in cluster 6 for both men and women, but it was also relatively high among men in cluster 4. These were the middle-class couples in which the men were typically the sole or the main earners. Their status as breadwinners may have given these men more confidence in money matters, while the women's lack of an independent income may have made it harder for them to get credit cards in their own right. Where a woman had a second card on her husband's credit card account, she might well hesitate before spending money on items of which he disapproved. A similar pattern existed in cluster 2, which contained a majority of couples in which the man was in full-time employment while the woman was in part-time work or did not have a paid job. The lower overall use of credit cards in cluster 2 reflects the fact that most of the men were in manual occupations, while cluster 4 contained a majority of men in non-manual occupations.

There were two clusters in which women were more likely than men to have made use of a credit card. The first was cluster 3, in which 40 per cent of women had used a credit card, compared with 33 per cent of the men. This was the cluster in which women tended to be better paid and better educated than the men, and this finding underlined yet again the importance of income and education in explaining credit card use. The second cluster in which marginally more women than men had used a credit card was cluster 5, which, as we have seen, contained the largest number of couples in which women were the main earners. This was also the cluster in which both partners were likely to be in full-time employment, with most of the men in jobs classified as skilled working class. Evidence from the focus groups suggested that this was a group in which many women felt confident with new forms of money, in a way that the men did not.

Perhaps the most striking finding to come from the cluster analysis was the importance of education. Making comparisons between the different clusters underlined the extent to which credit card use reflected not simply personal tastes and choices, but the economic context within which individuals and couples lived their lives. It might be expected that the use of credit cards would reflect economic variables such as income and employment, but it was surprising to see how important age at the end of full-time education seemed to be.

In order to examine the interacting effects of different variables, we carried out a multiple regression analysis, with the dependent variable being credit card spending.

The results of the regression analysis are reported elsewhere (Pahl and Opit, 1999). The regression analysis showed that, while total expenditure is related mainly to income, as might be expected, credit card expenditure is related to income and to age at the end of full-time education. People who were older when they ended full-time education tended to use credit cards more.

Table 7 highlights the main findings of the FES analysis by making comparisons between the extremes, in terms of income and education. It shows that credit card use varied greatly between low- and high-income women, low- and high-income men, and individuals with particularly short or particularly long educational careers. Of course, income and education were highly correlated. But there did seem to be a real 'education effect' which applied to both men and women.

The findings from the FES analysis were highlighted by an argument that broke out in one of the focus groups between two individuals who might be taken as speaking for clusters 1 and 6, respectively.

Table 7: Use of credit cards over a two-week period, by gender, income and education*

	% of women who used a credit card	% of men who used a credit card
Woman's income under £50 pw	16	21
Woman's income £600 pw and over	58	52
Man's income under £100 pw	10	10
Man's income £600 pw and over	63	68
Age at the end of full-time education 14 or less	9	14
Age at the end of full-time education 20 or more	48	60

Note: Total number = 3,767 couples.

Conflicting interests in the electronic economy

The argument occurred in a focus group composed entirely of men, and it began after Henry, a telecommunications consultant and an enthusiast for new forms of money, had dominated the discussion for some time. Jim, who was a retired headmaster from a disadvantaged part of the city, interrupted him:

> "The thing that worries me is that those people who don't want to move onto modern systems will eventually be penalised. Like standing orders – you may now get a discount if you operate one. And if you want to pay cash for your electricity you actually pay more. So you're penalised for trying to pay cash."

Interviewer: "How do you view the prospect of a cashless society?"

Henry: "It's a natural consequence of living We have got a credit card and I use it for buying things over the Internet. We don't like writing cheques – it's too much of a faff. We see it as very much an enabling technology in our house. My wife is a very independent lady. She uses telephone banking an awful lot. Now she's into Internet banking and most of our friends and acquaintances are like that."

This exchange is interesting in many different ways. The first speaker highlighted the penalties attached to remaining in the cash economy, while the second speaker was an example of the male technophile, for whom the electronic economy offers a wealth of new toys to play with, to the extent that he sees it as "a natural consequence of living." When Jim replied to Henry, he was thinking of all those people who live on social security benefits, paid through the Giro bank at the local Post Office.

"But there are hundreds and thousands of people who are collecting their Giro through the Post Office, handling cash much of which is already committed. They don't have these choices. All electronic banking is going to be of no use whatever and if there are penalties put on for actually dealing with cash we're going to have a further disadvantaged very large section of society."

Henry picked up the topic of people living on social security, but cleverly used it to advance his own argument. He referred to a recent proposal that social security benefits should be paid by means of a smart card. The aim would be to reduce fraud.

"But those same people, Jim, in two years time are going to get a card from the Benefits Agency. The Benefits Agency have plans to make every person who's in receipt of unemployment benefit – they won't get a Giro, they'll get a card like this. It might not be VisaCash. They just stick it in any cash machine, the system knows that they are due a payment and they've got the option to spend it or go to the bank and get their money."

In his reply Jim went back to the reality of life as he knew it, on a disadvantaged housing estate on the edge of a big city, and to the fact that many poor people find it easier to manage their finances in cash.

"They get this wonderful card to go to a wonderful machine, but that money's already heavily committed. It's hard enough having to divide it out to make it last, but an electronic system where you can't actually physically see the money.... And an awful lot of people still have the cocoa tin: there's the rent, there's the food, there's what I owe the club. An awful lot of people are not going to be able to handle it."

Conclusions

Both the quantitative and the qualitative data suggested an increasing polarisation between those who use new forms of money and those who do not, or cannot. The quantitative data were concerned only with credit cards, but it suggested clear patterns, which were confirmed, and illustrated, in the focus groups. While being in employment certainly affected credit card use, income and education seemed to be even more significant variables in determining whether or not individuals used a credit card to make a purchase. The importance of education underlines the point that access to the electronic economy involves being confident about acquiring the knowledge necessary to make best use of all the new forms of money; in the information society those who have been trained to access and manipulate information will surely be at a distinct advantage.

FIVE

New forms of money and financial arrangements within marriage

When two people marry, or begin living together, they create a new economic unit with its own financial commitments, such as the rent or mortgage repayment for the house in which they both live. Yet they also remain two separate individuals, who may have different levels of income and different priorities in spending. Every couple has to devise financial arrangements for making sure that joint bills are paid and that individual priorities are respected.

In this chapter, case studies from the face-to-face interviews will be used to explore the financial arrangements of married couples and to examine the use that they make, or do not make, of new forms of money. In order to create links with the previous chapter, case studies have been selected which reflect some of the ideal types that were identified by the cluster analysis.

A dual career couple using many new forms of money

Cluster 6 drew together a group of well educated individuals, in full-time jobs, whose incomes were relatively high by comparison with the rest of the sample, and who were classified as belonging to social classes I or II. Around two thirds of both men and women in this cluster had used a credit card during the two weeks of the FES survey.

Andrea and Michael were typical of cluster 6. Aged in their twenties, they both had degrees. They had no children and their full-time jobs as a tax consultant and a teacher gave them an income of just under £50,000 gross per year, or over £600 per week net. When shown a list of different financial arrangements and asked to pick the one that came closest to their own, both picked the system described as "We pool some of our money and keep some of it separately." As Andrea said,

> "We put an amount in every month from each of our personal accounts into the joint account. Then from the joint account

goes all the joint expenditure, like mortgage, bills, etc, etc. Then what is left in our own personal account is for our own use."

They had a credit card on the joint account in Andrea's name, for joint expenditure, and a number of other credit and debit cards for personal use. They used these cards for almost all their shopping and monitored spending carefully, paying the bills in full every month and never paying any interest. Michael described how this worked in practice:

"If it's a joint thing then we'd put it on her Barclaycard, and if it was business, it obviously comes off my business account, and if it's for going home to my parents, then I pay – that comes out of my money – and if we're going to her parents, then it comes out of her money. Presents? We each look after our own families."

Michael had a gold card and admitted that,

"Depending on who I'm with, if I want to vaguely impress them, I'll get out the gold card. If they get out their gold card, and we're splitting the meal fifty/fifty, then I whack mine on the table and that, er, gives some kind of credibility I suppose."

Neither used much cash and both were scathing about loyalty cards. Michael called them "a load of rubbish", while Andrea described them as:

"A con. I just think, you save thousands and thousands of points and then at the end of the month or whatever, they give you a voucher for five pence. I just think – why don't you just give me the money off the goods?"

They had thought about telephone and computer banking, but for the time being were satisfied with their existing arrangements. Their system enabled them to save and Michael was building up a portfolio of shares.

Previous research on money and marriage has developed typologies to describe the different ways in which couples control their finances (see, for example, Pahl, 1989; Vogler and Pahl, 1993). Andrea and Michael were using "partial pooling", a system characteristic of couples where both are earning. Their careful balancing of joint and separate spending represented the tension between their joint lives together and the expectations of their separate families of origin. Having enough money enabled them to use new forms of money to manage their finances and, on occasion, to impress others. Their situation was very different from that of the couples in cluster 1.

An unemployed couple with credit card debts

Cluster 1 in the previous chapter drew together a group of individuals who were typically dependent on state benefits, because they were either retired or unemployed. Tom and Teresa, aged 25, unemployed and with two young children, were finding it hard to make ends meet. Tom's Jobseeker's Allowance was paid into his bank account, while the payments for Income Support, Child Benefit and Housing Benefit were paid into Teresa's bank account. He gave her money towards the bills, but also liked to have something left to spend on hi fi equipment.

When asked about their financial arrangements, Tom and Teresa said, "We pool all our money and manage our household finances jointly", but in the separate interviews both said that Teresa was really responsible for making ends meet: when family income is low, women tend to get the job of making ends meet. Tom said, "I leave it all up to her". She said:

> "I have to remind him that there's things to pay and that he can't just go out and squander money. I get very worried about money, you see. If I haven't paid something I won't sleep. I have to pay my bills. And whatever I've got left I'll live on it. I can live on like a fiver a week, if I have to. But he says things like, 'We only live once'. You know, 'You're always going to get money'. But I think you have to pay bills to survive."

Tom explained his attitude in terms of his family of origin:

> "I'm not really money oriented. The family that I've been with hasn't really been money oriented. Whereas she, Teresa, should I say, she's from that different area and class. So she's got more responsibility with money than what I have. I'm quite glad she's there, because if she wasn't there, I'd spend all me money."

Their current financial problems were exacerbated by the fact that when she had been in work she had used her Visa card to pay for a holiday. They had taken out money up to and above her credit limit and were still paying off what they owed. She complained:

"I think it's ridiculous. I don't think you should have to pay interest on any cards or your accounts. They get enough money out of you as it is. I mean I've only got £500 over the limit and some people have got thousands and thousands on it."

Interviewer: "What do you feel when you're using your credit card?"

"I don't really know I'm doing it. Like I say, it's a piece of plastic and it's not like handing cash over. No, its plastic money. It's lies. You don't feel you're spending anything."

The interviewer asked Tom whether he was thinking of getting a new card:

"Um ... yes and no. 'Yes' because the simple fact is, like I say, it's as good as money, and you've got it on you whenever you need it. 'No' because there's sometimes you can overspend money, without knowing."

Interviewer: "What did you feel when you had a card and you used it?"

"I thought, 'Yeah, I've got this credit card here, and now I can go buy what I want, when I want'. Because I know, if I want something, that I will definitely get it. Most definitely."

Teresa and Tom were operating the system of financial management which in previous research has been described as "wife management" or the "whole wage system". This system is characteristic of low-income families. As in this example, the man's lack of involvement in financial matters can serve to protect his personal spending money and keep off the agenda the woman's struggles to make ends meet (Vogler, 1998). For Tom, new forms of money, such as credit cards, offer an opportunity for personal spending which may threaten the living standards of his wife and children.

The example of Teresa and Tom also raises a number of policy questions. What will happen when the Working Families Tax Credit is introduced, with the expectation that it will be paid with the wage earner's pay packet, unless the couple choose otherwise? Will it make it easier or harder for low-income couples to budget, especially if the man is the earner and the woman takes responsibility for managing finances, as is most often the case?

A breadwinner husband who controlled finances

A contrasting picture was presented by those couples who fell into cluster 4 in the previous chapter, which was typified by a middle-class breadwinner husband with a wife who had no paid work or just a part-time job. Derek and Helen fell into this category. He had left school at 18 and was an estate agent, while she had left school at 16 and now worked part-time in an office. They had three teenage children. There was a great disparity in their salaries, since she earned under £10,000, while he received at least £42,000 per annum gross, and may have earned much more, since this was the top point on the salary scale from which respondents were invited to identify how much they earned.

Both saw him as the main earner, and both considered that he controlled the family finances. They had a joint account, into which his salary was paid, while her salary was paid into her own account. She described how their system worked, and it was clear that, like many women in her situation, she did not feel comfortable about spending "his" money:

> "We have a joint account into which his money goes and the household expenditure is made from. So I'm very strict with myself about what I spend money from that account on. It won't be on things for me, because I have my own account for that. And it gives me a sense of independence to be able to do that."

Derek confirmed what she had said:

> "I mean, basically, I provide the money. She has her own independence now, but most of the money that comes into the household is mine. And the money that Helen earns, I don't touch at all. Dare I say absolute pin money or whatever. It's a bit of a chauvinistic statement that, but I'm not ashamed."

They had a joint Visa card, which was paid out of their joint account, and a joint debit card, and she had several store cards, which she paid from her own account. He also had an American Express card. In the past she had had her own Barclaycard, but did not pay off the outstanding debt each month. She described what happened:

"Derek said to me, 'Look, you're paying through the nose on your Barclaycard – really high interest rates. I'm going to get you transferred to the Cooperative Bank'. Well, I wasn't too keen, to be honest with you, because my Barclaycard I'd had since I was at work. So it was my sort of account, in my name. I didn't want to be second named on his account. Silly sort of thing really. So I sort of kicked my heels over this one for a little bit, cutting my nose to spite my face, and in the end sort of gave in. So now Derek gets the statements on our joint Visa card. Which in a way I don't really like, because he knows now what I'm spending with my credit card. I like to have some sort of mysteries in my life."

Her husband, in his own separate interview, described the same incident, but threw rather a different light on it:

"Helen was Barclaycard and she had about £1,500 on there. She was being charged 17% or 18%, which is dire. They were offering a freebie at the Coop, so I applied for a card, got her balance transferred over and they paid off the Barclaycard. Cut that up, and got rid of it at a special incentive rate of 6% for the first six months. I paid some of it for her, but I didn't pay the whole lot off, because – perhaps it's my thing – I've never discussed it with her as a discipline thing, that yes, I could pay it off, because I bring the money in. But it's important for Helen to contribute towards it, because she spent the money, you see."

The story of her credit card reflected a more general situation in which he ultimately controlled finances. When asked about making a major purchasing decision, she said:

"We would discuss it. But I would have to say, ultimately the decision would lie with Derek. And I think that boils down to the fact that he earns the money. It's as simple as that."

Helen had hinted that money was a way by which her husband sought to gain status: "He attaches a great deal to prestige. You know, to have a bank account with Coutts would be the ultimate; Barclays, Piccadilly, had to do us". And her husband corroborated what she had suggested:

"I mean I was in one of the most prestigious, well actually they've just sold it next to the Ritz – 160 Piccadilly, which is probably one of the ultimate banks. Then it got shifted to Regent Street, but Regent Street is only there on paper: it's actually in Shepherds Bush, which is a banking centre."

After talking to them both, the interviewer noted that "Points on loyalty cards meant monetary saving for her and an aid to budgeting. Points for him [American Express] meant gifts and luxuries, such as a trip to Paris".

Derek and Helen were operating the system of financial management described in previous research as "male controlled pooling", but with a strong ideology of the male as breadwinner, which is reflected in his control of finances and Helen's feeling that she has no right to spend "his" money on herself. The dispute about her credit card illustrated his power to control the discussion (Vogler, 1998).

This couple underlined the point that two individuals living in the same household can have access to different amounts of money, can vary in their right to spend that money, and can have different standards of living. They may also keep secrets from each other.

Financial strategies and secrets within marriage

Both the interviews and the focus groups produced many examples of the financial strategies and individual secrets that can exist within marriage. There is only space here to summarise some of the main themes that emerged.

Maintaining financial independence can be a strategy by which individuals protect their spending from surveillance by their partner. It most often occurs in situations where both partners have broadly similar income levels, as was the case with Andrea and Michael. Couples who are cohabiting are also more likely to maintain independence in their financial affairs than married couples. For example, among the focus group participants, seven of the 11 people who were part of a cohabiting couple said they maintained independence in financial matters, compared with none of those who were part of a married couple.

Female financial management continues to be the preferred strategy by which lower-income couples aim to make ends meet, as was the case for Teresa and Tom. This pattern is now well-documented (see, for example, Goode et al, 1998). However, new forms of money have created additional hazards and temptations for those who are not strong willed, and wives may find themselves bearing the brunt of the frustration created by exclusion from the electronic economy.

The longstanding association between *money* and *power* has extra potential when money can take so many different forms. In a world where people shop for the best bargains in money, or where some types of money confer greater prestige than others, there are new possibilities for those who have more money than others. The effect may be to exacerbate inequalities both within households and between households. Both Derek and Helen explicitly made links between money and status, and some of the focus group discussions developed into a power struggle between participants over who was most knowledgeable about new forms of money.

The *power of the breadwinner* continues, but may be expressed in rather different forms. One focus group contained a man who preferred cheques, because filling in the stubs provided a record of spending. However, his wife preferred credit cards. She was about to give up her job, and he said:

> "She's more inclined towards the credit card type of thing – Barclaycard. She's always done it that way. I'm more conscious of getting into debt, but she's got a different outlook on that. I'm loath to pay interest on them and I think the interest builds up.... I have to rein her in a bit. I'll be inclined to put a hold on it because the money is all coming out of the same pot."

> *Interviewer:* "I was going to ask you, do you have joint accounts, separate accounts?"

> "Well, we've always had separate accounts, but now with her not working we are actually closing her account. Because I'm the main earner, so it's me that has to keep an eye on that. I do all the sorting out of domestic finances."

> *Interviewer:* "So what's going to happen to the Barclaycard?"

> "Now all of that will have to stop and it will have to be channelled through my income. She won't have a bank account. We won't get a joint account, there's no point. There's nothing coming into it from her side." (Man around 40, job centre manager)

Different norms about the use of credit can cause problems between couples. One woman said that:

"Because of Christmas it has just been a nightmare. He has started a college course which he has to pay £300 before Christmas, which is a hell of a lot out of his wage. Because mine is like a little job, so it is not bringing in a proper wage, as I call a proper wage. And finding that extra money that would be spent on Christmas presents for the kids, it is hard. You see the way he looks on it, we have held back a bit because he gets paid on 22nd December. So I have to go then and finish all the Christmas shopping, which is like a nightmare."

Interviewer: "Is this not where a credit card would come in...?"

"He would not let me have it. He said 'You are not using a credit card because we can't afford to pay for it'. I can't see the kids going without a Christmas present, yet he won't let me use the Visa to go and buy them. So tempers are a bit high at the moment."

Another participant: "I would have hit him on the head and go and use it."

"But he is the main earner and the bills have to be paid ... it's difficult." (Woman aged 31, part-time sales assistant)

The introduction of new forms of money can make *secrecy a strategy* for individual married people. In one focus group a woman described how:

"We have a joint credit card, but I won't use that 'cos it has to be paid, the whole balance, every month, and I can't afford to pay the whole balance every month. So I done a bit of a sneaky one and I got a Barclaycard. Well, he cut up my Barclaycard and said I couldn't have it and then he found out that I'd renewed it. He found it in my purse and he went, 'What's this?' Now I have my own credit card; that's my debt. So my money that I have separately from him, I have to pay that myself: that don't come from our money."

Interviewer: "So how do you decide what's our money, my money and his money?"

"Well, we both get paid into the bank and my money pays the mortgage and all the bills, then his money is so much housekeeping in cash, and the rest of it we split down the middle and that's my spending money for the week. And then out of my spending money for the week I have to pay for my credit card and whatever else I wanna do, go out or whatever." (Woman aged 39, part-time secretary)

The record provided by the credit card statement can make it harder to have secrets:

"I've had a credit card before and run up to the limit on it and not been able to pay it off every month. Every month I'd got nothing left by the time I'd paid off what I owed. So I've got one now, but it's my husband's credit card if you like – I'm an additional cardholder. So he in a way knows everything I'm spending on it. I just think if I only used cash I wouldn't have done that, but its easy if you're not careful to get carried away." (Woman aged 34, complaints officer for BT)

Conclusions

This chapter has examined some of the ways in which new forms of money are being incorporated into the financial systems of couples in Britain. It is still early days in the development of the electronic economy, but already some trends are emerging. New technologies seem to be having a polarising effect, giving privileges to those who are already privileged, and creating new traps and hurdles for those on lower and less secure incomes. Within marriage, new forms of money may be altering the balance between "our" money and "my" money, diminishing collective imperatives and allowing individuals to pursue their own financial goals without consulting their partners. All these changes have implications for social policy in its widest sense.

SIX

Banking in the electronic market-place

Over the last quarter of the 20th century, the world of retail banking has changed dramatically. New ways of doing business, new outlets and new products have been launched into what had been a very traditional and conservative part of the high street. How have the customers responded? Banking is located at the heart of the economic system, and it might be expected that economic rationality would dominate the decisions that individuals make about their banks. But is this the case?

In both the focus groups and the individual interviews, participants were invited to talk about their current banking arrangements, about the choices that they had made and the reasons for those choices. Their answers suggested that economic motives were by no means paramount when individuals and couples made decisions about banking. However, before turning to the new data, it may be helpful to have a brief overview of the changing world of banking.

The changing world of banking

The changes that are taking place in banking are highly interrelated. However, there are a number of distinct themes that can be identified within the larger story. These include the deregulation of the financial services sector, the extension of banking outlets and the creation of new financial products; underpinning all these changes are the developments that are taking place in information technology.

Developments in information technology are both a cause of, and a consequence of, changes in banking. A report on the partnership between IT and banking began:

> Technology is a dynamic force. As it becomes an increasingly vital element in the competitive landscape of the financial service industry, technology is changing the very nature of selling and delivering financial products. (Gandy and Chapman, 1996, p 1)

Gandy and Chapman went on to argue that, just as bankers face the certainty that technology will influence developments in the banking industry, so technology firms have come to realise that banking is one of the largest and most sophisticated markets for their products.

The use of new technologies in banking has gone through a number of different stages. In the first stage, centrally-managed mainframe computers were used to automate processes such as cheque handling and to reduce back office costs. In the next stage, the development of more flexible and distributed computer systems made it possible to carry out financial operations in real time, and so to provide services such as automatic teller machines (ATMs), debit cards and telephone banking. The most recent stage has seen the development of client/server systems in which data can be held centrally, while services such as home banking can be made available on user-friendly programs held on personal computers.

The changes have affected the internal workings of banks, as well as the services available to their customers. So the 'back office', where cheques are handled and accounts kept, has become increasingly automated and centralised. At the same time, the 'front office' has seen fewer bank tellers providing a personal service, and more machines at which customers can withdraw cash, pay in cheques and monitor the state of their bank balances. Table 8 sets out the different stages of the changes that have taken place and lists some of the applications that they have made possible.

Table 8: Technological change and banking applications

Decade	Processing methodology	Banking applications
1970s	Batch processing on mainframe computers	Faster cheque handling; automated accounting; lower back office costs
1980s	Real-time and on-line computer systems	Automated teller machines; credit and debit cards; authorisation processes; telephone banking
1990s	Client/server public access networks	Home-based banking; customer-oriented front offices; customer information systems; micro marketing techniques; centralised back offices

Source: Adapted from Gandy and Chapman (1996, p 11)

The changes that have taken place underline the fact that banking is essentially concerned with information handling. Banking is less and less dependent on the high street branches and is more and more a matter of the electronic exchange of information about money. This raises the question of the bank of the future:

> Without branches what exactly is a bank? It becomes nothing more than a conductor of transactions, a facility which might equally well be undertaken by the telecoms corporations or on-line service providers. (Gosling, 1996, p 59)

In the debate about the future of banking, there are many different scenarios. In one scenario the telecoms industry could become a major provider of financial services, since it already controls the necessary infrastructure and the customer data base. In another scenario the providers of on-line computer services could move into banking, especially if and when the majority of homes are linked to the Internet. A poll in January 1999 showed that nearly a third of adults in Britain had access to the Internet, either at work or at home; however, access was unevenly distributed, with middle-class men aged 25–34 being most likely to be connected and, semi-skilled and unemployed people least likely (*The Guardian*, 11 January 1999, p 1). In another possible scenario, and one that is already underway, the banks are in partnership with the major supermarkets (Brown-Humes, 1998b). As we shall see from the focus groups and interviews, some of the banks' customers seem to trust supermarkets more than banks when it comes to providing financial services.

The development of *new financial outlets* followed from the deregulation of the financial services sector in the 1980s. This made it possible for building societies to offer services comparable to those provided by the high street banks, and for other retailers, such as Marks and Spencer, Sainsbury's and Tesco, to offer financial services for the first time. The fact that these services are actually organised in partnership with the traditional banks is not widely publicised. For example, one focus group participant compared the financial services provided by Tesco and the National Westminster Bank, apparently unaware of the fact that the two are in partnership: "In much the same way that Tesco offers own-brand baked beans, but sources them from a specialist, so the arrangement is replicated with banking" (Gosling, 1996, p 61).

The combination of new outlets and new technology has led to a reduction in the numbers of high street branches maintained by the traditional banks. This process has been exacerbated by the decline of the high street and the move to out-of-town shopping centres, catering for the car-owning shopper. With ATMs giving customers access to their accounts in supermarkets, hospitals, universities, stations and airports, and with telephones and computers making it easy to bank from home or work, the high street branch is surely under threat.

The withdrawal of branch banks from the poorer parts of cities is another part of the same trend. As other outlets proliferate, as branches become relatively expensive to run and as banks become more profit-conscious, providing services for poorer customers becomes increasingly unattractive. Nearly 3,500 bank branches have been closed since 1990 and the inner cities have been particularly badly hit (Waugh, 1999). One commentator said:

> The writing is clearly on the wall for branches in poorer areas. Notwithstanding the USA's Community Reinvestment Act of 1977, branches in low profit, poor areas are closing in both the US and the UK. Banks have made it increasingly clear that they have no moral obligation to operate branches as a community duty. Their primary duty is, after all, to make profits. (Gosling, 1996, p 34)

The effect has been to exclude some individuals and communities from a wide range of financial services, or to make such services more expensive:

> People without bank accounts face charges for cashing cheques or making payments through post offices, and are unable to take advantage of reduced tariffs for paying bills on direct debit. (Kempson, 1996, p 174; see also Kempson, 1994)

One possible alternative is the credit unions, which offer low-cost loans to poorer people while giving reasonable interest on deposits; but at present credit unions are limited in what they can provide. It is important that social policy analysts widen their field of interest to consider the ways in which specific policy interventions can extend access to financial services (Conaty and Mayo, 1997).

The development of **new financial products and services** is another part of the revolution; indeed, it is significant that banks and banking are increasingly seen as part of a wider 'financial services sector'. The financial services offered to the ordinary citizen now include not just bank accounts and bank loans, but also ATM cards, credit cards and debit cards, insurances, mortgages, advice on investments and pensions, share dealing and currency exchange. The picture is complicated by the fact that many of these services are offered not just in banks, but in supermarkets, post offices, building societies and other locations. The proliferation of radio and television programmes, popular magazines and articles on the subject of personal finance can be seen as evidence of the dazzling variety of what is on offer. In the pages that follow the term 'bank account' will be used to cover both bank and building society accounts.

A very useful review of research on financial services and on consumer attitudes, preferences and perceptions has been provided by Lewis et al (1997). They suggested that financial consumers are becoming more demanding, less loyal and better informed, but that the 'personal touch' remains important, especially for older customers. However, they warned that the increasing complexity of financial services is matched by increasing complexity in family arrangements, with more divorces, remarriages and non-traditional family forms than ever before. They concluded by suggesting that it will be important to explore attitudes to new financial services in the context of family structure, life-style and culture (Lewis et al, 1997, p 6). With this in mind, we turn to the evidence that came from the focus groups and interviews.

Focus group comments on changes in banking

Members of the focus groups were invited to discuss the changes in the world of banking. Developments in information technology often proved to be a contentious issue, as we saw in Chapter 4. Some individuals clearly enjoyed the changes that are occurring in the financial services sector and took pride in being up-to-date, whereas others were more or less reluctant to adapt to the changes.

Among the 59 people who took part in focus groups, 12 were currently banking by telephone. This cannot be taken as representative of the population as a whole, because one group was composed entirely of people who banked by telephone. Typically, men were more likely to be banking by phone than women, and people in middle-class occupations much more likely than those whose occupations were classified as working class. The same patterns in reverse emerged among those who were not currently using telephone banking, with women being twice as likely as men to express doubts about the idea, and working-class people being more suspicious and less well-informed.

Those who were actually using telephone banking were enthusiastic. They liked being able to contact the bank at any time, not having to queue, being met with a helpful and pleasant response, and being spared the journey to the bank or the need to write a letter. The reasons given for not banking by phone, in order of the frequency with which they were given, were the lack of face-to-face contact, the impersonality of the telephone, problems involved in remembering the password, antagonism to being kept waiting and a general sense that banking was not something that people wanted to do in their leisure time and at home: as one man said, "You're doing the work for 'em'."

Banking by computer attracted less interest than telephone banking, but the patterns were the same, with men tending to be more interested than women. This finding is in line with international data which show that male dominance in the use of the Internet occurs in every country for which information is available (Singh, 1998a, 4). The main concern among the sceptics was the security of computer held systems, while a typical enthusiast said, "You've got more control − you've just gotta click and up it comes".

Participants in the focus groups were also interested in new banking outlets. Some people lamented the demise of the traditional high street branch bank:

> "Years ago you used to know who the bank manager was, and now it's just a load of young women. You've got a 'personal banker', but it's never the same one for long." (Woman aged 39, secretary)

But others felt that the high street banks had exploited their customers and were keen to find alternatives:

> "The thing with banking, it's all going to change so much. Now Tesco's are into it, Sainsbury's are going in, Virgin, he's going into it: now you can bet your life that Richard Branson'll do a good deal." (Man aged 53, transport planner)

Many people, like the man above, did not seem to realise that supermarket banking involved partnerships with the high street banks. Other complaints about the high street banks included the lack of personal attention, high charges, long journeys to the bank, and the risks involved in getting money from ATM machines. One woman, who used her debit card for everything, including getting 'cash back' at the supermarket, concluded:

"I used to quite like going into that bank; they were always very friendly. But they've closed it down now. I don't think I'll ever go into a bank again." (Woman aged 49, practice nurse)

There was also interest in new financial products and services, though often knowledge on this topic was extremely patchy. It seemed as though some people were shopping around to get the best bargain in money, just as they shopped around for bargains in other goods. This approach was often tempered with a degree of resentment about the time and effort involved in 'shopping for money'. Some individuals were enthusiastic about the bargains to be derived from loyalty cards and air miles schemes, while others were irritated by the way in which these schemes added to the pile of cards in their wallet.

However, running through all the focus group discussions was another, more complex, discourse, which was essentially about the ways in which banking arrangements grew out of and reflected the intimate relationships of the people involved. When it came to planning the interviews, this became an important focus.

Couples and their banking arrangements

The interviews included a series of quite detailed questions about banking arrangements. Since each partner was interviewed privately, it was then possible to compare the answers that the man and the woman gave to the same questions. This sometimes produced some very different views on the same topic.

Only one man, out of the 80 who were interviewed, claimed never to have had a bank account. He was an unskilled worker, who was paid in cash and who had a longstanding mistrust of banks:

"Don't believe in them. What I have I keep in my pocket; I can feel it there; I can see it there. As I says, I like me beer, come home and drink it, and then I go to sleep. And that's about it. Never trust banks and I never will."

The fact that he had not filled in the self-completion questionnaire suggested that he might be illiterate, and this is a reminder of the financial barriers faced by people who cannot read and write. Exclusion on the grounds of low income can be compounded by the exclusion that comes from lacking the functional literacy needed to open an account, fill in a cheque or read a credit card bill.

One reason that he could manage without a bank account was that his wife was in charge of finances in the household. She was also paid in cash, but had opened a bank account in order to be able to take out a loan and pay direct debits. However, she still preferred cash:

> "I just like the money in my hand. I'm lazy really. I can't be bothered like to write these cheques out and keep account of what I've paid."

Evidence from the Family Resources Survey suggested that in 1996, 23 per cent of adults in Britain did not have a current bank account (ONS, 1998, p 105). Around 1.5 million households, or 7 per cent of the population, lack even the most basic of financial products, such as a current account and home contents insurance; another 10 per cent have just one financial product, most commonly either a current or a savings account in a bank or building society (Kempson and Whyley, 1999, p 4).

However, for most of those who were interviewed, banking was an accepted part of life, and they described a bewildering mix of joint and individual accounts. In the literature on banking, relatively little is written about the choice between joint and sole accounts (see for example, Gosling, 1996 and Burton, 1994). However, in the interviews it became clear that couples attached great significance to this issue. A similar finding emerged from the study of marriage and banking carried out in Australia by Singh. She reported that between 71 and 83 per cent of married couples had joint accounts at the time, and concluded that, "the personal joint account, more than any other single mechanism, makes visible the marital couple as the domestic financial unit" (Singh, 1997, p 42).

The figures for this study are very similar with 29 (73 per cent) of the 40 couples having at least one joint account. The pattern of account holding for the 40 couples is set out in Table 9. Eight couples only had joint accounts, but a more common pattern, followed by 21 couples, was to have a mix of joint and sole accounts. It was surprising to see that women were more likely to have these sole accounts than men, but the reasons for this emerged when the interviews were analysed in more detail.

Table 9: Types of account held by the couples who were interviewed*

| | No sole accounts | One or more sole accounts | | |
		Woman only	Man only	Both partners
One or more joint accounts	8	10	1	10
No joint account	–	1	1	9

Note: Total number = 40 couples.

Eleven couples did not have any joint accounts. In two cases this was because one partner or the other was reluctant to have any involvement with banks at all. However, in nine couples both partners had separate accounts, without any jointness in their banking arrangements. This model, which also emerged in the focus groups, was more often found where couples were cohabiting, rather than being married, or where there were no children.

The pattern of account holding was reassuringly similar in the focus groups and the interviews, so that in both data sets half of the couples had both joint and sole bank accounts, one quarter of the couples had only joint accounts, and one quarter only had sole accounts.

The 40 couples who were interviewed were between them responsible for around 150 bank and building society accounts. This total is not apparent in Table 9, where multiple accounts are not recorded. Many joint account holders had several such accounts, usually because they had both a current and a savings account. The largest total was achieved by the couple who had one joint account, four sole accounts in her name, and 16 accounts in his name, in order to take advantage of any bonus payments made by demutualising building societies!

At first it was difficult to make sense of the mass of detail about banks and bank accounts. However, reading the interview transcripts, it became clear that people's replies to the questions about banking revealed as much about their biographies, and about past and present relationships, as they did about their use of financial services. From this observation came the idea of 'banking as biography'. A similar result emerged from the research that Singh carried out in Australia. Her original research question was, "How has deregulation changed the relation of banks and consumers?" However, she was surprised to find that most of her interviewees did not mention the issue of deregulation until she brought it up. She was forced to conclude:

I was asking about changes in banking, but they were talking about how they handled money in their marriage. (Singh, 1997, p 30)

Singh's research underlined the significance of the different ways in which couples managed their finances and drew attention to the importance of looking at banking and new forms of money. She suggested that banking arrangements can provide a way of understanding the broader patterns of money management used by a couple. Table 9 shows that just over half of the couples had both joint and sole accounts. In terms of the existing literature on family financial arrangements, this would be classified as 'partial pooling' (Laurie and Rose, 1994; Laurie, 1996). However, what did 'partial pooling' mean to the people concerned? In an attempt to answer that question, we shall consider two rather different couples.

Banking as biography

Daniel and Rosie were an example of a couple whose financial arrangements were a reflection not only of their past experience, but also of their current situation and their aspirations for their relationship. Both were in their thirties. Daniel was an executive with a major company, earning over £60,000 per year, while Rosie's work as a part-time art teacher brought in about £8,000. She described the way in which they managed their money as: "we pool some of our money and keep some of it separately", while he described their system as "we keep the money separate but manage it jointly".

Rosie's banking arrangements revealed quite a lot about her biography. She said:

"I've got this joint Abbey National account with Daniel that I use but he doesn't use at all: that's in my married name. I put my Child Benefit into that account and my salary and I use it for childcare and everyday household expenses. And I've got an Abbey National Savings account in my maiden name: if I had money left over, or if my father gave me a cheque, I'd put it in that account rather than the joint account. I've got a current account with Lloyds Bank, which I've had since I was 17: I hardly ever use it, but I keep it in case I want to do a direct debit. Then I've got a Post Office National Savings account which is in my maiden name: that used to be for postal orders from Godmother and things like that: so I don't draw on that, obviously. Also I have an account still in Paris because I lived in Paris for two years: I haven't used that for years."

Daniel's banking arrangements were evidence of a very different life. He had three accounts, all with First Direct and all in his sole name, and he moved money between them regularly. He had a current account with First Direct, out of which he paid all the household bills, and from which Rosie's credit card was paid automatically by direct debit. His other accounts included:

"... a high interest savings account, which has a penalty on withdrawals, so I keep a sum of money in there which I don't draw on; when I have a surplus at the end of the month in my current account I transfer across to the high interest account as much as I can. And I have another savings account which has slightly lower interest. I keep about a thousand pounds in that little account: if I travel abroad I pay for air tickets and hotels with my American Express Gold Card and then the company repays that into my account to reimburse me."

Daniel was very concerned that his much larger income would not become a problem in their relationship. He remembered his father sitting paying bills by cheque and glorying in his role as the breadwinner for the family:

"I don't want to control her in the way that I've seen my father control my mother. I don't want to feel in control or wield any power – although obviously I do because I earn the majority of the money. But we make it less important by never discussing it and things just automatically go out of my account. It's not something we would talk about openly, but I'm quite sure it's there as subtext to some of the problems we have in our relationship. Because obviously my work has to take something of a priority because of the prominence of my income in our everyday life."

For Daniel, telephone banking helped him to conceal his dominant financial position from Rosie. She was not sure how often he contacted the bank: "It's difficult to be sure if he's dealing with all that stuff – but I overheard him speaking on the phone the other day because one of his accounts had been paid twice". He said that he phoned the bank about every two weeks: "Checking all balances, paying accounts – I can do it from my desk and I can do it at home – terrific". However, despite all his efforts to maintain equality, and his belief that financial decisions were made jointly, Rosie was in no doubt that he was ultimately in control of finances in the family.

Banking as a map of a relationship

Sarah and Simon were an example of a couple whose banking arrangements seemed like a map of their past and present relationships. Both were in their fifties and for both this relationship had come as a fresh start after many years of marriage and child rearing. Financial disputes in their previous marriages had made them both aware of what could go wrong, so they were determined that this time money would not become a problem. Figure 2 sets out their bank accounts and the flows of money for which they were responsible.

Figure 2: Banking arrangements as a map of family realationships (£ per month)

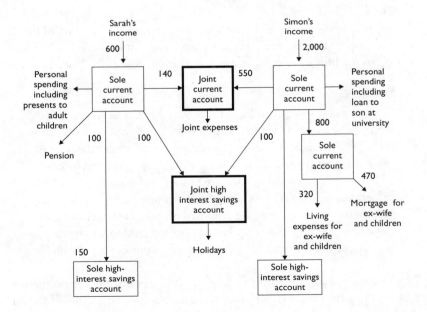

Sarah explained that they had set up this financial system because:

> "We both have individual responsibilities. Simon has his family and I have mine. I also have various savings. I have my family responsibilities, things that traditionally I've done and I wanted to go on doing. It seemed the most equitable way of coming together, sharing."

She explained how the system worked in practice:

> "My income goes into my sole account and £140 goes into our joint account to cover our joint expenses. Then £100 goes into our joint deposit account, £150 goes into my high income savings account, £100 goes into my pension, and there's a bit left for me: I never quite know how much is left. So I have two purses: I have the joint account purse, with the joint account Switch card, and then my purse – it's got my money in there."

Simon made comparisons with the financial arrangements that applied in his parents' house and in his first marriage:

> "My father was the sole earner and he gave my mother a housekeeping allowance. My father's attitude was you should never have a joint account because no one person's responsible and you can't be sure that you are going to manage the account properly. So when I got married I didn't have a joint account. My wife had certain areas of expenditure, food, children and children's clothes, and I had some areas, like the household bills, but there wasn't any pooled money."

Interviewer: "Why did you change and do it differently with Sarah?"

> "I think I did it differently because I wanted to do two things. I actually wanted to recognise myself as independent and I also wanted to recognise that we were doing a partnership, so having a pool and having my own seemed to reflect what I was doing."

He explained how the system worked:

> "My salary goes into my main account. One big block of £800 goes into a second cheque account which is used for all the expenses

to do with my kids: that's £470 for the mortgage payments and the life policy and £320 into [ex-wife's] account, all on standing orders. And then £550 goes into my joint account with Sarah, that's for the Council Tax, food and other household expenditures. Then we have a high interest savings account for holidays and we put £100 into that. And then I've got a savings account of my own – I sold my books and the income from that I put into a savings account, that's in my name, and if at the end of the month I have surplus in my main account, it goes in the savings account. I gave my son a one-off loan for his university things and he's paying me back."

However, feelings were as important as logic:

"When I joined up with Sarah, the fact of my being overdrawn was a matter of anxiety to her, so the fact that I am now in control of my money is actually important in our relationship. If my money got out of control then I think that would be a point of contention. We both recognise that money has a powerful dynamic in our relationship. I think it's important to have a shared pot and our own bits, but also being in control of however much money we have is quite symbolic, like being in control of life in a sense."

This example underlines the complexity of financial arrangements in families where divorce and remarriage mean that family financial obligations may be spread across several households. The patterns that can emerge have been documented by Burgoyne and Morison (1997). The implications for policy, especially in terms of child support and the distribution of property on divorce, are enormous.

Conclusions

This chapter has shown that understanding changes in the banking arrangements of couples depends as much on understanding the changing nature of marriage as it does on knowledge about new technologies and changes in banking outlets and products. The issue of control is central to both family finances and banking.

Both the focus groups and the interviews produced evidence of dissatisfaction with traditional forms of banking. Most people had bank accounts, but for some closures and amalgamations had reduced accessibility. In this context it is very significant that the Financial

Services Authority may be given the power to insist that banks have a duty to counter financial exclusion and that the Financial Services and Markets Bill may include legislation on local access to financial services (Waugh, 1999). 'Community banks' and credit unions may provide some solutions to the problem of access to banking for poorer people.

The joint account continues to be a powerful symbol of marital togetherness, but an increasing concern with financial autonomy is showing itself in the growth of 'partial pooling', where couples combine joint and sole accounts. Women are more likely than men to have sole accounts, because they:

- may have their earnings paid into a sole account in order to give them some financial autonomy when the man's larger salary goes into a joint account;
- may have their earnings paid into a sole account to reflect its status as 'treat money' for the family, while his earnings go into the joint account for the main bills;
- may have an account into which housekeeping money is transferred;
- are more likely to keep accounts open for sentimental reasons, such as pleasure in past income, even though little or no money is now earned.

Every couple that sets up home together has to find a way in which to strike a balance between the individual and the couple, between being two financially autonomous beings or one financial unit with joint bills to pay. In this process, economic rationality may be less important than ideologies about the nature of marriage and norms about family finances. Banking arrangements, as they record financial history and map the pattern of past and present relationships, offer a powerful guide to understanding wider issues within the changing patterns of marriage and family life.

SEVEN

The implications for social policy and for financial services

The financial lives of individuals are located on the crossroads between the state and the market, between the public and private sectors. On the one hand, the state regulates the financial situation of every citizen, through the tax system, the social security system and a myriad of other controls on wages, salaries, interest rates and prices. On the other hand, the financial services sector epitomises the free flowing nature of market capitalism in a global economy; any interference by policy makers is likely to be seen as threatening the efficient working of the system.

In this context, making proposals for policy is a dangerous enterprise. However, it is clear that social policy analysts cannot any longer ignore the implications for welfare of financial services, information technology and shopping (Cahill, 1994). The findings presented in this report suggest that there are many questions that policy makers might consider.

Financial exclusion

This study has underlined the continuing reality of financial exclusion, as it applies both to credit and to banking. Some individuals and households are much less likely than others to use credit cards, one of the main forms of credit for most of the population. Those who are poor, unemployed or elderly are less likely to use credit cards than those who are in employment; and, except when they are in full-time employment, women are less likely to use credit cards than men. Those with fewer years of education are less likely to use credit cards than those with more education.

In a consumer society, access to credit is becoming an important aspect of welfare. Credit allows individuals to smooth out the peaks and troughs in their income and to purchase those goods and services they require, even when they do not have enough money to pay for them. However, it is clear that some individuals and some households are excluded from the mainstream credit-based society; if they do use credit it tends to be from more expensive sources (Kempson, 1994; Rowlingson, 1994; Rowlingson and Kempson, 1994). In a consumer society, the poor too easily become defined as 'flawed consumers', to use the phrase coined by Bauman (1998).

The implications of financial exclusion are now well documented (Kempson and Whyley, 1999; Molloy and Snape, 1999). Those who are at the highest risk of financial exclusion include people on low incomes, those claiming means-tested benefits, those who left school before the age of 16, those living in rented accommodation, members of the Pakistani or Bangladeshi communities and those living in the most deprived local authorities. The issue has been a focus for the government's Social Exclusion Unit and for Policy Action Team 14, and there are currently a number of public and private sector initiatives aimed at reducing exclusion. It will be important that the reports and recommendations coming from these initiatives are acted upon.

The current revival of interest in credit unions is to be welcomed. A *credit union* is "a cooperative society offering its members loans out of the pool of savings built up by the members themselves" (Berthoud and Hinton, 1989, p 1). The aim is to provide accessible credit at reasonable rates of interest to groups based on a locality or a workplace, and to give people a sense of taking control over their finances. Britain has a much less well developed system of credit unions than some other countries, despite attempts by local authorities to encourage them (Berthoud and Hinton, 1989; Leyshon et al, 1993). This is largely because of the restrictions imposed by the 1979 Credit Unions Act, which prevents credit unions from giving unsecured loans for more than two years, caps loans at £5,000 above what a member has saved and limits membership to a maximum of 5,000 people.

The recent consultation document proposes lifting the present limit on the numbers of members, extending the loan repayment period and allowing credit unions to offer other financial services (Brown-Humes, 1998d). It is important that these recommendations are translated into legislation at an early date. It is also important to explore other routes to extending credit to low-income individuals and households. In the USA the Community Reinvestment Act imposes an obligation on banks to endeavour to meet the credit needs of their local communities (Oppenheim, 1998, p 177). This is interesting as an example of using the private sector to meet the needs of those who cannot themselves afford to use private sector services.

Future developments in the electronic economy

The study suggested that future developments in the electronic economy are likely to increase the gap between the privileged and the excluded. Telephone and Internet banking will be available only to those with the technology, the education and the confidence to use them. Smart cards potentially offer a route into electronic money for those without the financial standing necessary for acceptance by the major credit card companies. However, they will become widely accepted only when they are issued without charge and when there are sufficient outlets for them to be used for most types of shopping.

The experiment in Swindon with the Mondex card may have ended in failure, but VisaCash seems to have proved reasonably successful in Leeds when the focus groups and interviews took place there. Smart cards are being used in many workplaces, such as universities, to purchase everything from food and drink to photocopying, and it seems likely that they will be used in the future to carry health records, replace passports and driving licences, and as membership cards for a range of leisure activities (Brown-Humes, 1998c).

A proposal to pay out benefits by means of smart cards has recently been shelved. The aim was to cut down on fraud, but there was concern that such cards could cause problems for some claimants. This study has shown that unemployed and retired people are much less likely than other groups to use credit cards, and more likely to use cash as their main form of money. Some find it hard to budget with the "invisible money" that is made available to them in the form of the credit limit on their card. If social security benefits came on a smart card, many would simply turn the payment into cash and work with that.

There seems to be a gap between the perspectives of those who provide and those who use the electronic economy. The discourse of providers is couched in terms of economics, efficiency and competition, while users, as this study has shown, are more concerned with social relations and cultural values. One study of electronic money concluded:

> The challenge is to find a language which can connect the economic analysis of supply and demand, cost and price, with the sociological study of access and use, trust and meaning. (Singh, 1998b, p 25)

In any future debates, it will be important for providers and policy makers to be aware of the very different perspectives of different groups of users.

Financial education and advice

The study underlined the importance of education in giving people the skills and the confidence to use the electronic economy. The focus group discussions and interviews revealed how much people varied in their knowledge about financial services. Some could discuss the advantages and disadvantages of different products and were enthusiastically "shopping for money", while others knew little about even everyday forms of money. It was also clear from the focus group discussions that some people were less well informed than they thought they were: in particular, those who were credit-poor were more likely to be information-poor.

Basic literacy and numeracy are likely to be increasingly important; and, as personal financial services extend into new fields and become more complex, there will be an urgent need for accessible information. The popularity of money advice programmes on radio and television, and the ranks of magazines about personal finance in every newsagent, are evidence of the growth of interest. Some schools already include finance in their curriculum, but education on some aspects of finances would seem to be an essential component of education for citizenship. However, it has to be recognised that some people are simply not interested in money, in the issues with which this report is concerned, or in the whole paraphernalia of the consumer society. To demand that everyone undertake education in consumer matters may be to impose undue costs on individuals.

The Financial Services Authority has been given responsibility for providing appropriate information and advice to consumers of financial services. It has been suggested that this be done in partnership with other organisations, drawn from industry, central and local government, advice agencies, educational institutions, trade unions and the media (Financial Services Authority, 1998; National Consumer Council, 1999).

The growth of the information society offers new opportunities by which information can be made available. More widespread provision of open access to the Internet would serve two functions: it would enable individuals to make use of the information and financial services available on the net, and it would also increase their confidence in using computers.

Understanding money and marriage

This study has underlined the point that a married or as-married couple cannot be regarded as a single economic unit. There were significant differences between men and women in terms of their access to credit, their use of credit cards and their attitudes to money and budgeting. Full-time employment was important in giving women access to a wider range of financial services and the confidence to use those services; women in part-time employment or without paid work could be in a very different financial situation from their partners.

There are many ways in which the assumption persists that a married couple is a financial unit. When building societies were demutualised, many wives found that they had no right to the one-off payments made to account holders, since payments went to the first name on the account, and the use of the conventional term 'Mr and Mrs X' meant that the payment went to the man, even in situations where the woman had originally set up the account. The whole debate about social exclusion tends to ignore the fact that a married woman, especially one without paid employment, can be more 'excluded' than her husband.

Money continues to be seen as male territory, especially among the more affluent, and this can make women increasingly disadvantaged. The technophilic enthusiasts for new forms of money were predominantly male. The development of Internet banking and shopping is likely to be led by those who have the greatest interest in computing, which is typically the man of the household. The man who keeps the accounts for the couple on his computer spreadsheet has more power in financial matters than the woman, who simply gives him the information to enter on that spreadsheet.

The study suggested that new forms of money may be changing and individualising the financial arrangements of married couples, but that, despite this, men are still finding ways to exercise control over the finances of the household. This may not be a problem when both partners are in full-time employment, but when the income of one partner falls, for example, when the woman gives up paid work to have a baby, the result can be an increase in financial inequality. The 1996 Family Law Act has made significant changes to the process of obtaining a divorce or separation, in particular setting up a system of mediation, information-giving and reflection, before the divorce can be finalised. All those who are concerned with giving advice to married or divorcing couples should be aware of the different economic positions of men and women within marriage and of the implications of changes in the electronic economy for individuals and families. New forms of money may be changing the ways in which couples manage their finances, but they are also reproducing, and in some cases reinforcing, some very traditional inequalities within and between households.

Appendix A: Methods of the study

Money is a sensitive and private subject. All researchers know that asking people about their finances can be more intrusive than asking about sexual relations. In addition, this study was essentially exploratory. Therefore it seemed important to use a variety of research methods, partly in order to throw the investigative net as widely as possible, and partly to gain experience about the acceptability and validity of different methods, in a way that might benefit future research on the topic.

Three different sources of data were used, in order to gain both quantitative and qualitative information about the issues that were being explored. First, analyses of the Family Expenditure Survey provided quantitative data about 3,676 couples, which could be generalised to a larger population because of the nature of the survey. Second, seven focus groups took place, involving 59 individuals living in five different parts of England. Finally, 40 face-to-face interviews were carried out, in order to develop a more qualitative understanding of the ways in which individuals and couples managed their finances and made use of new forms of money.

The Family Expenditure Survey

The Family Expenditure Survey (FES) is a long-running continuous survey, carried out by the Office for National Statistics (ONS), using a random sample of households drawn from every part of the United Kingdom. Interviews take place in about 7,000 households every year, and involve all 'spenders' over the age of 16. The survey collects information about the income and expenditure of the household as a whole; in addition, each individual spender is asked to complete an expenditure diary over a two-week period. We used the data set that was collected in 1993/94, when the response rate was 70 per cent (ONS, 1996).

When they complete the FES expenditure diary, respondents are asked to list every single item they have bought and to note whether a credit card was used to make the purchase. This means that the FES is a rich source of data about credit card use, but it cannot tell us anything about the use of debit cards, cheques or other means of handling money.

Since the study was concerned with family finances and with the spending patterns of individuals and couples, the re-analysis began by selecting households containing a married couple. The FES does not identify stable cohabiting couples, so unfortunately these could not be included in the analysis; also excluded were households where the 'head of household' was under 20. This gave us a total of 3,691 couples, or 7,382 individuals. However, there were a few cases in which crucial data were missing, so the total sample used here numbered 3,676.

The data derived from the expenditure diaries were recoded in order to make the analysis more manageable. There were some 315,633 entries in the diaries kept by the couples who were the focus of the analysis, and in the raw data set they had been classified by the FES into several hundred expenditure categories. We recoded these to produce a total of 37 major categories, ranging from food, motor vehicles and household goods, which were the largest items in the diaries in terms of amounts spent, to clothes, holidays, gambling and alcohol. The recoding involved grouping linked items together. So the category 'motor vehicles' included not simply the purchase of cars and motor bicycles, but also petrol, vehicle insurance, tax, repairs and other running costs; the category 'household goods' included purchases of bedding, furniture, carpets, kitchen appliances, lamps and clocks.

It is important to remember that many items of household expenditure were not recorded in the diaries because they were paid by direct debit or standing order out of bank accounts; these included payments for mortgage or rent, for Council Tax and for utilities such as water and electricity. Some people paid these by cash, cheque or credit card and noted them in their diaries, but since many did not these items were excluded from the analysis.

The re-analysis also made use of the wealth of socio-economic information contained in the FES, and especially the information about age, employment, household composition, education and social class. In some cases these data too were recoded in order to produce summary variables. In particular, we were interested in the impact of employment, income and educational level on the use of credit cards by men and women within these households.

The focus groups

The aim of the focus groups was to learn something about the meanings that people attach to different forms of money and to explore variations in those meanings for different groups of the population. The focus groups were organised by Social and Community Planning Research (SCPR), with the help of a recruitment agency. Focus group participants were recruited according to predetermined quotas, in order to achieve a balance in terms of age, sex, employment status and geographical area. In all, seven focus groups were held, during the winter of 1996-97, with 59 individuals taking part. All the focus group discussions were tape recorded and transcribed verbatim.

The focus groups varied in terms of their location and their composition, as follows:

Swindon, Wiltshire: five men and five women, aged 26-38

Reading, Berkshire: four men and five women, aged 42-53

Broxbourne, Hertfordshire: three men and four women, aged 29-55, no credit cards

Broxbourne: four men and four women, aged 26-49, all banking by phone

Leeds, Yorkshire: eight women, aged 26-42

Leeds, Yorkshire: eight men, aged 30-60

Birmingham: nine women, aged 30-49

Swindon was chosen because, since 1995, MasterCard had been carrying out an experiment with the Mondex smart card, offering cards to local residents and supplying the necessary terminals to local outlets. As the study progressed another experiment began in Leeds, in 1997, with the issuing of the VisaCash card, so two groups were held there. Both Mondex and VisaCash were chargeable cards, and could be used to pay for newspapers, car parking and drinks in the pub as well as larger items.

In terms of age, the focus group participants ranged between 26 and 60, with 26 participants aged under 40, 31 aged over 40 and two whose ages were not known. All the participants were currently living as one of a couple, with 11 cohabiting and the rest being married. However, only one member of each couple attended the focus groups, so evidence about differences between the partners was essentially one-sided. In all, 35 women and 25 men took part.

There was a spread in terms of employment status among focus group participants, and in terms of the extent to which they used new forms of money. In 26 couples both partners were in full-time employment; in 21 couples one partner, usually the man, was in full-time employment while the woman had a part-time job; in 11 couples the man was in full-time work while the woman was out of paid work, usually because of her responsibility for small children; finally, there was one couple where the woman was the sole earner.

The discussions that took place within the focus groups were led by a facilitator, who followed a topic guide, but allowed some flexibility in the time spent on particular issues. Headings in the topic guide included changes in dealing with money, using cash, bank accounts and building societies, credit cards and debit cards, loyalty cards, telephone banking, computer banking and chargeable cards. Depending on the composition of the group, other topics might be covered, but all the groups ended with a discussion of how new forms of money were changing the financial arrangements of couples.

Those who attended the focus groups cannot be treated as representative of the population as a whole. Since the focus was on the financial arrangements of couples, all the participants were living as one of a couple, and so older and younger people were under-represented and there were no single people, though many talked about the financial arrangements they had had when they had been single. Compared with the population as a whole there were relatively few unemployed people: this reflected the fact that most participants were selected because they used credit cards, except for those in the one group whose members had never used, or were currently not using, credit cards. Finally women were over-represented among the participants, with 35 women compared with 24 men: this reflected the fact that two women-only groups were selected, compared with just one men-only group.

The focus groups produced a wealth of information and ideas about how people use new forms of money and about how family financial arrangements are adapting to the electronic economy. Some of the gaps in the ranks of the focus group participants were filled when the respondents for the interviews were selected.

Face-to-face interviews

The face-to-face interviews were designed to explore in more detail the ideas that had come from the focus groups. Data were collected in three different forms. First, the recruitment agency recorded information about marital status, employment and age on the original recruitment questionnaire. Second, each interviewee filled in a self-completion form giving details of education, income, patterns of spending, use of new forms of money, financial decision making and financial arrangements. Third, each partner was interviewed privately, using a topic guide similar to that used for the focus groups.

Interviewing both partners separately and privately was an important part of the research design. There is now a considerable body of evidence to show that husbands and wives may have very different perspectives on the same issue: "his marriage" can be very different from "her marriage" (Bernard, 1982). The focus groups had revealed considerable differences between partners in their feelings about, and use of, new forms of money, and we wanted to explore this in more detail. All the interviews were tape recorded and transcribed. The result was a complex data set in which it was possible to compare the different perspectives of men and women and to examine in detail the ways in which they spoke about the different forms of money they used.

A recruitment agency was used to find the interviewees. With such small numbers, it did not seem sensible to try to assemble a random sample of the general population; moreover, the aim was to build on the results that had come from the analyses of the FES. So the recruitment agency was asked to select couples on the basis of quotas in terms of employment status, age, social class and geographical location. These were the characteristics that had been particularly significant in the analyses of the FES.

In terms of employment status, the spread was similar to that in the general population. In eight couples both partners were in full-time employment; in 10 couples the man was in full-time employment while the woman had a part-time job; in nine couples the man was in full-time work while the woman was out of paid work, usually because of her responsibility for small children; in three couples both partners were unemployed; while in 10 couples both partners were retired. In terms of social class, 22 of the women and 23 of the men had occupations classified as A, B or C1, while 14 of the women and 16 of the men had occupations classified as C2, D or E; one man and four women could not be classified in terms of their social class. The ages of those who were interviewed ranged from 22 to 72.

Since two of the focus groups had taken place in Leeds, eight of the interviews also took place there. The remainder took place in different parts of London. With such a small number of interviews, it did not seem sensible to attempt to cast a wider net in terms of geography.

Conclusions

Using a number of different methods in research is described technically as 'triangulation'. The hope is that each method will reveal a different aspect of the topic being investigated and that the result will be greater understanding than could be gained by the use of just one method.

The strength of the FES consisted in the numbers of people involved and in the amount of detail provided about the spending patterns of each individual: this was a randomly selected sample and very large data set, from which it was possible to make generalisations about the wider population. The weakness of the FES was that it gave no information about the motives and feelings of the people involved.

The focus groups created a vivid impression of how people talked and felt about new forms of money, and they gave rise to some quite heated debates. However, each group developed its own dynamic, so that what individuals said was shaped as much by group dynamics as by their own personal experience; in addition, though everyone who took part in the focus groups was married or living as-married, there was no way of checking whether their partners would have given the same account of the couple's finances.

The interviews redressed the balance, by collecting data from both partners, using the same set of questions with each. The results revealed that husband and wife could have very different perspectives on money, but the small numbers involved meant that it would be dangerous to generalise from this data set. Taken together, the three methodological approaches gave a robust account of how couples in England in the late 1990s were using a variety of new forms of money.

Appendix B: The cluster analysis

Previous analyses had suggested that the use of credit cards was statistically associated with a number of different personal, demographic and financial characteristics of the individuals in the sample. Clearly, such variables were interrelated in a complex way. A clustering technique was used to create a new classification of individuals which could use the collinearities between individual educational attainment, individual income and the joint employment characteristics of the sample. The new classification was then compared with the earlier model based on the joint employment categories. The aim was to identify clusters of individuals with common characteristics and to investigate patterns of credit card use for each cluster.

Methods of the analysis

The method used was K clustering (SPSS), with the number of clusters being 6, so that there was a correspondence with the number of joint employment categories used in earlier analyses. The procedure was carried out separately for the men and the women in all 3,676 couples. The individual clusters were then characterised in terms of a typical representative, and the proportion of each cluster that made some credit card expenditure within the two–week period was calculated. The following recoded variables were used for the cluster analysis.

The joint employment groups were recoded into three categories, so that:

FT/FT and FT/PT (ie two earners)	1
FT/no paid work and woman main earner (ie one earner)	2
both unemployed and retired (ie no earners)	3

The gross income per week of the man was recoded into seven categories, so that:

£0–100	0
£100–200	1
£200–300	2
£300–400	3
£400–500	4
£500–600	5
Over £600	6

The gross income per week of the woman was recoded into seven categories, so that:

£0–50	0
£50–100	1
£100–150	2
£150–200	3
£200–250	4
£250–300	5
Over £300	6

Age at the end of full-time education was recoded for both men and women, so that:

age 14 or under	1
age 15	2
age 16	3
age 17–19	4
age 20 plus	5

Results of the analysis

In order to examine the interlocking effects of the different variables, the programme was then invited to define six clusters, using the recoded variables. The results are shown in Table B1.

Table B1 shows that **cluster 1** contained 965 women and 979 men. Typical representatives of this cluster had ended their education at 14 or 15. Incomes for both men and women were low, while a high proportion of these households had no earners. Relatively little was spent by credit card.

Table B1: Cluster analysis of FES data on credit card (CC) use*

| | Cluster | | | | | |
	1	2	3	4	5	6
Women						
Number in cluster	965	916	332	515	659	289
Age at end of FT education	1.63	3.09	3.95	3.27	2.63	4.12
Woman's income recoded	0.41	0.58	5.14	0.82	2.8	5.2
Man's income recoded	0.63	2.03	1.9	4.88	1.86	5.04
HH employment cats recoded	2.79	1.66	1.32	1.6	1.26	1.14
Mean amt spent on CC in two weeks (£)	8.03	15.06	43.81	55.4	24.59	105.11
Men						
Number in cluster	979	872	298	533	713	281
Age at end of FT education	1.55	3.02	3.42	3.62	2.58	4.18
Woman's income recoded	0.14	0.53	5.36	0.89	2.78	5.26
Man's income recoded	0.61	2.07	1.9	4.85	1.85	5.04
Joint employment cats. recoded	2.77	1.68	1.31	1.58	1.28	1.14
Mean amt spent on CC in two weeks (£)	10.71	22.74	42.64	90.41	16.28	105.88

Note: * See Chapter 4 for a description of the clusters.

Cluster 2 contained 916 women and 872 men. Education had lasted longer in this cluster, and the typical age at the end of full-time schooling was 16. Men's incomes were higher than in cluster 1 and there was a bigger gender difference in income levels. The relatively high scores for the joint employment categories suggested that many of these households had either one earner or no earners, while the income variable suggested that their incomes were low. Credit card spending was low compared with other clusters, especially for women.

Cluster 3 contained 332 women and 298 men. Education was more prolonged in this cluster, especially for women, many of whom had stayed on at school to 17 or 18. Women's incomes were among the highest in the whole sample, which suggested that in many of these households women were the main earners. By contrast, men had relatively low incomes.

Cluster 4 contained 515 women and 533 men. Education levels were relatively high, especially for men, with most individuals staying on at school until 16–18, and this was reflected in higher income levels. The big gender gap in terms of income, and the relatively high scores for the joint employment categories, suggested that many of these households had only one earner, and followed the 'traditional' pattern of breadwinner husband and homemaker wife. Spending on credit cards was high, by comparison with other clusters.

Cluster 5 contained 659 women and 713 men. Educational levels were relatively low here, with most people leaving school at 15 or 16. Incomes were low, especially for men, while the low scores for the joint employment categories suggested that most of these households had two earners: they could be described as 'work-rich', except that the jobs they did were so low paid. Credit card spending was low compared with other clusters, especially for men.

Cluster 6 contained 289 women and 281 men. A typical representative of this cluster had completed some form of higher education. The effect of this showed in the relatively high income levels for both men and women. The relatively low scores for the joint employment categories suggested that both partners were in paid work: these were the 'dual-career' couples, or the 'work-rich'. The amount spent by credit card, by both men and women, was by far the highest for the sample.

Confirmation of the patterns indicated by Table B1 came from examining the clusters in terms of the social class of the 'head of household', which was defined by the FES in terms of the Registrar General's classification of the occupation of the man in each couple. The results, presented in Table B2, showed that in cluster 6 social classes I and 2 predominated; cluster 5 contained more skilled manual workers (social class 3M) than any other social class; cluster 3 was spread more evenly across the social classes but had larger proportions of social class 2 and skilled manual workers.

Table B2: Six clusters by percentages in each social class

Social class	Cluster number					
	I	2	3	4	5	6
I	0.5	3.6	7.7	18.9	3.5	30.6
II	3.0	16.6	33.2	44.3	18.9	52.3
III non-manual	2.0	8.3	10.4	10.7	8.6	7.5
III manual	11.4	39.7	21.1	15.0	38.3	3.9
IV	5.7	13.8	7.4	3.4	13.9	1.4
V	3.2	3.9	2.3	0.8	4.3	0.4
Not recorded	74.1	13.8	17.4	6.0	12.9	3.6
Total number	979	872	298	533	713	281

Note: Social class classified by class of 'head of household'.

Total numbers = 3,676 couples

Table B2 also threw light on the variations between couples where the man was the main or sole earner. As we saw in Table B1, cluster 2 contained many individuals who ended their full–time education at the age of 16 and whose income was correspondingly low; it is likely that many of these women had young children and that having no paid work, or only part–time work, was a temporary phase in their lives. By contrast, in cluster 4 the men tended to be more educated than the women, and men's incomes were among the highest in the sample; these couples might be characterised as 'traditional' couples, where many women did not have a paid job but concentrated on home making, while the man played the role of breadwinner. These patterns were confirmed by an examination of the social class of the man in each couple, shown in Table B2. In cluster 2 skilled manual workers (social class 3M) were the largest single group, while in cluster 4 social classes 1 and 2 predominated.

Comparison of Tables B1 and B2 underlines how much is lost by classifying social class in terms of the 'head of household'. This archaic practice assumes that the occupation of the man sets the tone for the life of the household. However, the analyses presented here, and in the main text, showed how much households varied when the education, income and employment of both partners was taken into account.

References

Bauman, Z. (1998) *Work, consumerism and the new poor*, Buckingham: Open University Press.

Beck, U. and Beck-Gersheim, E. (1995) *The normal chaos of love*, Cambridge: Polity Press.

Begg, D., Fischer, S. and Dombusch, R. (1994) *Economics*, London: McGraw-Hill.

Bernard, J. (1982) *The future of marriage*, London: Yale University Press.

Berthoud, R. and Hinton, T. (1989) *Credit unions in the United Kingdom*, London: Policy Studies Institute.

Berthoud, R. and Kempson, E. (1992) *Credit and debt*, London: Policy Studies Institute.

Brannen, J. and Wilson, G. (1987) *Give and take in families: Studies in resource distribution*, London: Allen and Unwin.

Brito, D.L. and Hartley, P.R. (1995) 'Consumer rationality and credit cards', *Journal of Political Economy*, vol 103, no 2, pp 400-33.

Brown-Humes, C. (1998a) 'All ringing, all dancing', *Financial Times*, 18-19 July.

Brown-Humes, C. (1998b) 'Banking in the aisles', *Financial Times*, 16 May.

Brown-Humes, C. (1998c) 'Where smart money is headed', *Financial Times*, 11 July.

Brown-Humes, C. (1998d) 'Movement seeks a loosening of law's shackles', *Financial Times*, 16 November.

Burgoyne, C. and Morison, V. (1997) 'Money in remarriage: keeping things separate – and simple', *Sociological Review*, vol 45, pp 363-95.

Burton, D. (1994) *Financial services and the consumer*, London: Routledge.

Cahill, M. (1994) *The new social policy*, Oxford: Basil Blackwell.

Cheal, D. (1992) 'Changing household financial strategies', *Human Ecology*, vol 21, pp 197-213.

Cole, G. (1999) 'All-in-one but not one-for-all', *Financial Times*, 23 February.

Conaty, P. and Mayo, E. (1997) *A commitment to people and place: The case for community development credit unions*, London: New Economics Foundation.

Credit Card Research Group (1997) *Cards on the Continent*, London: Credit Card Research Group.

Credit Card Research Group (1998) *What's on the cards?*, London: Credit Card Research Group.

Crook, J.N., Thomas, L.C. and Hamilton, R. (1994) 'Credit cards – haves, have-nots and cannot-haves', *Service Industries Journal*, vol 14, no 2, pp 204-15.

Duca, J.V. and Whitesell, W.C. (1995) 'Credit cards and money demand – a cross-sectional study', *Journal of Money, Credit and Banking*, vol 27, no 2, pp 604-23.

Equal Opportunities Commission (1997) *Briefing on women and men in 1997*, Manchester: Equal Opportunities Commission.

Feinberg, R.A., Westgate, L.S. and Burroughs, W.J. (1992) 'Credit cards and social identity', *Semiotica*, vol 91, pp 1-2, 99-108.

Financial Services Authority (1998) *Promoting public understanding of financial services: A strategy for consumer education*, London: Financial Services Authority.

Ford, J. (1988) *The indebted society: Credit and default in the 1980s*, London: Routledge.

Ford, J. (1991) *Consuming credit: Debt and poverty in the UK*, London: CPAG.

Forester, T. (1987) *High-tech society*, Oxford: Basil Blackwell.

Gandy, A. and Chapman, C. (1996) *The electronic bank: Banking and IT in partnership*, London: Chartered Institute of Bankers.

Goode, J., Callender, C. and Lister, R. (1998) *Purse or wallet? Gender inequalities and income distribution within families on benefits*, London: Policy Studies Institute.

Gosling, P. (1996) *Financial services in the digital age*, London: Bowerdean.

Graham, G. (1997) 'Cash still preferred for small payments', *Financial Times*, 9 June.

Hine, C., Eve, J. and Woolgar, S. (1997) *Privacy in the electronic marketplace*, Uxbridge: Brunel University.

Inman, P. (1999) 'Slow on the uptake for smart cards', *The Guardian*, 22 July, p 27.

Kempson, E. (1994) *Outside the banking system: A review of households without a current account*, London: HMSO.

Kempson, E. (1996) *Life on a low income*, York: Joseph Rowntree Foundation.

Kempson, E. and Whyley, C. (1998) 'Financial exclusion', Paper presented at the Joseph Rowntree Centenary Conference held at the University of York.

Kempson, E. and Whyley, C. (1999) *Kept out or opted out?: Understanding and combating financial exclusion*, Bristol: The Policy Press.

Kempson, E., Bryson, A. and Rowlingson, K. (1994) *Hard times: How poor families make ends meet*, London: Policy Studies Institute.

Laidler, D. (1993) *The demand for money*, London: Harper Collins.

Laurie, H. (1996) *Women's employment decisions and financial arrangements within the household*, PhD Thesis, University of Essex.

Laurie, H. and Rose, D. (1994) 'Divisions and allocations within households', in N. Buck, J. Gershuny, D. Rose and J. Scott (eds) *Changing households: The British Household Panel Survey 1990-1992*, Colchester: University of Essex.

Leyshon, A., Thrift, N. and Justice, M. (1993) *A reversal of fortune: Financial services and the South East of England*, London: Seeds.

Lewis, A., Betts, H. and Webley, P. (1997) *Financial services: A literature review of consumer attitudes, preferences and perceptions*, Bath: University of Bath School of Social Sciences.

Mackintosh, J. (1998) 'How to make a net saving', *Financial Times*, 18-19 July.

McCloskey, D. (1987) 'Fungibility', in J. Eatwell, M. Milgate and P. Newman (eds) *The new palgrave: A dictionary of economics*, London: Macmillan.

Molloy, D. and Snape, D. (1999) *Low income households: Financial organisation and financial exclusion – A review of the literature*, London: DSS.

Morris, L. and Ruane, S. (1989) *Household finance management and the labour market*, Aldershot: Avebury.

National Consumer Council (1999) *Financial Services and Markets Bill: Response to the Treasury's Consultation on the Draft Bill*, London: National Consumer Council.

ONS (Office for National Statistics) (1996) *Family Expenditure Survey*, London: HMSO.

ONS (1998) *Social Trends 28*, London: HMSO.

Oppenheim, C. (1998) *An inclusive society: Strategies for tackling poverty*, London: Institute for Public Policy Research.

Pahl, J. (1989) *Money and marriage*, London: Macmillan.

Pahl, J. (1995) 'His money, her money: recent research on financial organisation in marriage', *Journal of Economic Psychology*, vol 16, no 3, pp 361–76.

Pahl, J. and Opit, L. (1998) *Cluster analyses of credit card use in the Family Expenditure Survey*, Canterbury: Department of Social and Public Policy, University of Kent at Canterbury.

Pahl, J. and Opit, L. (1999) 'Patterns of exclusion in the electronic economy', in J. Bradshaw and R. Sainsbury (eds) *Researching poverty, vol 2*, Aldershot: Ashgate.

Rowlingson, K. (1994) *Moneylenders and their customers*, London: Policy Studies Institute.

Rowlingson, K. and Kempson, E. (1994) *Paying with plastic: A study of credit card debt*, London: Policy Studies Institute.

Singh, S. (1997) *Marriage money: The social shaping of money in marriage and banking*, St Leonards, NSW, Australia: Allen and Unwin.

Singh, S. (1998a) *Gender, design and internet commerce*, Centre for International Research on Communication and Information Technologies, Melbourne, Australia: RMIT University.

Singh, S. (1998b) *Understanding the use of electronic money: The missing factor in policy*, Centre for International Research on Communication and Information Technologies, Melbourne, Australia: RMIT University.

Treas, J. (1993) 'Money in the bank', *American Sociological Review*, vol 58, pp 723-34.

Treasury Select Committee (1999a) *Third Report: Financial services regulation*, HC 1998-99 73-I, London: HMSO.

Treasury Select Committee (1999b) *Third Report: Financial services regulation*, HC 1998-99 73-II, London: HMSO.

Vogler, C. (1998) 'Money in the household: some underlying issues of power', *Sociological Review*, vol 46, no 4, pp 687-713.

Vogler, C. and Pahl, J. (1993) 'Social and economic change and the organisation of money in marriage', *Work, Employment and Society*, vol 7, no 1, pp 71-95.

Vogler, C. and Pahl, J. (1994) 'Money, power and inequality within marriage', *Sociological Review*, vol 42, no 2, pp 263-88.

Waugh, P. (1999) 'Banks for the poor may have to re-open', *The Independent*, 22 February.

Wilson, G. (1987) *Money in the family*, Aldershot: Avebury.

Wilson, V. (1999) *The secret life of money*, St Leonards, NSW, Australia: Allen and Unwin.

Winnett, A. and Lewis, A. (1995) 'Household accounts, mental accounts and savings behaviour', *Journal of Economic Psychology*, vol 16, no 3, pp 431-48.

Wolf, C. (1998) 'Time to cook the books', *Sunday Times*, 25 October.

Worthington, S. (1998) 'Retailers and financial services in the United Kingdom', *Journal of Financial Services*, vol 2, no 3, pp 230-45.

Zelizer, V. (1994) *The social meaning of money*, New York, NY: Basic Books.